FINANCING TOMORROW'S INFRASTRUCTURE
CHALLENGES AND ISSUES

Proceedings of a Colloquium
October 20, 1995

Board on Infrastructure and the Constructed Environment
Commission on Engineering and Technical Systems
National Research Council

NATIONAL ACADEMY PRESS
WASHINGTON, D.C. 1996

NOTICE: The Board on Infrastructure and the Constructed Environment (BICE) is a continuing activity of the National Research Council (NRC) and advises the executive and legislative branches of government and the private sector on questions of science, technology and public policy related to above ground and underground construction; public facilities; infrastructure systems and services; the relationship between the constructed and natural environments and their interaction with human activities; and related issues of planning, design, construction, management, and use of the built environment.

The National Academy of Sciences is a private, nonprofit, self-perpetuating society of distinguished scholars engaged in scientific and engineering research, dedicated to the furtherance of science and technology and to their use for the general welfare. Upon the authority of the charter granted to it by the Congress in 1863, the Academy has a mandate that requires it to advise the federal government on scientific and technical matters. Dr. Bruce Alberts is president of the National Academy of Sciences.

The National Academy of Engineering was established in 1964, under the charter of the National Academy of Sciences, as a parallel organization of outstanding engineers. It is autonomous in its administration and in the selection of its members, sharing with the National Academy of Sciences the responsibility for advising the federal government. The National Academy of Engineering also sponsors engineering programs aimed at meeting national needs, encourages education and research, and recognizes the superior achievements of engineers. Dr. Harold Liebowitz is president of the National Academy of Engineering.

The Institute of Medicine was established in 1970 by the National Academy of Sciences to secure the services of eminent members of appropriate professions in the examination of policy matters pertaining to the health of the public. The Institute acts under the responsibility given to the National Academy of Sciences by its congressional charter to be an adviser to the federal government and, upon its own initiative, to identify issues of medical care, research, and education. Dr. Kenneth I. Shine is president of the Institute of Medicine.

The National Research Council was established by the National Academy of Sciences in 1916 to associate the broad community of science and technology with the Academy's purposes of furthering knowledge and of advising the federal government. Functioning in accordance with general policies determined by the Academy, the Council has become the principal operating agency of both the National Academy of Sciences and the National Academy of Engineering in providing services to the government, the public, and the scientific and engineering communities. The Council is administered jointly by both Academies and the Institute of Medicine. Dr. Bruce Alberts and Dr. Harold Liebowitz are chairman and vice-chairman, respectively, of the National Research Council.

Funding for this activity was provided through an agreement between the National Academy of Sciences and the National Science Foundation, Award number CMS-9505733, the U.S. Department of Commerce/Economic Development Administration, Award number 99-07-13779, the U.S. Department of Commerce/National Institute of Standards and Technology, Award number 43NANB510831, the National Science Foundation, Award number CMS-9633297, and the U.S. Department of Commerce/National Institute of Standards and Technology, Award number 43NANB611071.

Library of Congress Catalog Card Number: 96-69107
International Standard Book Number: 0-309-05543-1

Additional copies of this report are available from: National Academy Press, 2101 Constitution Avenue, NW, Box 285, Washington, D.C. 20055
800-624-6242 or 202-334-3313 (in the Washington Metropolitan area)

Foreword

The mission of the Board on Infrastructure and the Constructed Environment (BICE) is advise the government and private sector on matters within the scope of its charter that are of national interest. The national infrastructure is an essential underpinning of our economy and quality of life and is a source of both serious problems and opportunities. BICE is committed to reaching out to all parts of the infrastructure community by fostering a dialogue among experts from various fields to identify issues and contribute to their resolution.

There are two basic issues concerning the infrastructure: how to make the infrastructure more efficient and affordable and how to finance it. The first issue was the subject of a colloquium held on March 24, 1995, that was focused on the challenges of providing future infrastructure in a changing and unfamiliar environment. The proceedings of that colloquium, *The Challenges of Providing Future Infrastructure in an Environment of Limited Resources, New Technologies, and Changing Social Paradigms*, are available from the National Research Council.

The second issue—how to finance the infrastructure—is particularly critical at this moment because federal appropriations are, at best, going to remain at current levels, but will probably decrease. Thus it will fall more and more to state and local governments and members of the private sector to come up with innovative and creative ways to address this critical issue.

This publication represents the proceedings of a colloquium, held on October 20, 1995, at the National Academy of Sciences, entitled *Financing Tomorrow's Infrastructure: Challenges and Issues*. The colloquium was an attempt to explore these issues in a social, political, and financial context, to examine models for successfully financing infrastructure projects, and to discuss new and innovative ways of dealing with contemporary realities.

The opinions presented herein are solely those of the authors of the colloquium papers and do not represent the opinions or position of the Board on Infrastructure and the Constructed Environment, the National Research Council, or the National Academy of Sciences. These proceedings are offered by BICE as part of a series of outreach activities for discussing critical infrastructure issues.

Contents

I. OVERVIEW 1
    George Bugliarello

BALANCING PRESENT COSTS AND FUTURE BENEFITS 7
    Timothy J. Brennan
Public Policy toward Private Infrastructure Investments, 8
Public Projects: Resource Flows and Money Flows, 9
Borrowing from Ourselves, 10
Why Financing Matters, 11
Should We Build and for Whom?, 13
Discounting, 14
Equal Standing: Adding Ethics to Economics, 15
Ethical Justifications for Discounting, 17
Final Word to the Present, 18
Discussion, 18

II. INFRASTRUCTURE CHALLENGES AND ISSUES: A PANEL............21
    Nancy Connery

DOMESTIC AGENDA..22
    Carol Everett
House of Representatives Report, 23
Economic Policy Institute Report, 25
U.S. Army Corps of Engineers Report, 25
Conclusion, 26

INTERNATIONAL PERSPECTIVE..28
    Frannie Humplick

CURRENT ISSUES IN INFRASTRUCTURE FINANCE........................39
    Natalie R. Cohen

DISCUSSION OF THE MORNING PRESENTATIONS........................45

TECHNOLOGY, INFRASTRUCTURE, AND COMPETITIVENESS IN
A NATIONAL INNOVATION SYSTEM..54
    Deborah L. Wince-Smith
National Technology Innovation System, 56

Financing Innovation, 61
Regulatory Obstacles, 63
Role of the National Laboratories, 65
Conclusion, 66

III. FUTURE OF INFRASTRUCTURE FINANCE 67
    Bruce D. McDowell

    DULLES GREENWAY: PRIVATE PROVISION OF TRANSPORTATION
    INFRASTRUCTURE 68
    Charles E. Williams
    Discussion, 72

    FLEXIBILITY IN INFRASTRUCTURE FINANCE...............................76
    Richard Mudge
    Discussion, 81

    PERSPECTIVE OF THE INVESTMENT COMMUNITY 84
    Ann L. Sowder
    Discussion, 90

    SOLUTIONS FOR LOCAL GOVERNMENT 95
    Paul S. Tischler

    BIOGRAPHICAL SKETCHES OF COLLOQUIUM
    PARTICIPANTS...102

List of Tables and Figures

TABLES
1   Responsibilities for Infrastructure Provision under Alternative
     Financing Arrangements, 32
2   Value of Infrastructure Privatizations in Developing Countries, 37

FIGURE
1   Publicly Guaranteed Private Loans Have Fallen, 30

Overview

George Bugliarello
Polytechnic University

In the course of this colloquium, some clear messages have emerged about the future of financing infrastructure, both in this country and abroad. The realities of the straitened financial picture with regard to infrastructure were reflected in talks by all of the panelists about what is possible right now. Far from being pessimistic, however, the panelists presented some new information and profound insights detailing influences that will have a great impact in the future. These influences must be better understood to be managed effectively and enable us to respond to changing conditions.

Dr. Brennan discussed the key public policy issue in infrastructure investment, i.e., deciding to commit resources to a particular project or program rather than how to finance it. Dr. Brennan emphasized that resource flows are more important than money flows. On that basis, the present preoccupation with budget deficits (which relate to money flows) as a justification for reducing infrastructure investment (resource flows) may be misplaced. He presented a tutorial on the potential consequences of these decisions indicating that how infrastructure is financed, although not the most essential issue, may indeed matter a great deal.

Dr. Brennan presented two points of view on how to balance present value with future benefits, an "opportunity cost" and an "equal standing" approach, for deciding for whether or not to make investments. But he also pointed out that decisions also have an ethical, or even philosophical, basis. He pointed out that the dictates of the market, or what we actually *do* in markets, do not always reflect what we *should* do or what we might want to do. We may decide, for example, to intercede in the market for reasons of public interest or to prevent monopolies.

The complex relationship between economic and ethical considerations is underscored by Hume's Law—what "is" is not necessarily what "ought" to be. Dr. Brennan discussed various ways of assessing the interests of future generations—from discounting them entirely to arguing for equal justice in the distribution of resources, which would target the generation we think will be most in need of help. The issue of intergenerational equity is fundamental, he noted. The way we value the interests of future generations, typically through market rate discounting, has a profound impact on the equity of decisions we make today.

In the ensuing discussion, it was pointed out that we had not addressed what could be called "intracontinental" equities. But the fact is that this country has been able to afford things that few other countries have been able to afford. Few other countries have been able, for example, to rebuild in a different area of the country, as we have essentially done by transferring people and resources from the east to the west. One could expand this principle to the problems of American cities, although the situation is, perhaps, not unique to the United States. Our cities have two distinct characters, daytime and nighttime. The question is whether or not our cities can become whole again. The answer may lie in telecommuting and other technological innovations. Another issue about urban centers mentioned in the discussion is that putting resources into highways takes resources away from city transit systems, making transportation for workers in the city less accessible.

The morning panel on infrastructure challenges and issues, chaired by Ms. Connery, also raised a number of important points. Ms. Everett suggested that we consider new roles for the state, local, private, and federal sectors in the context of national strategies and objectives, a point that was reinforced by the keynote luncheon speaker, Ms. Wince-Smith. Ms. Everett cited three recent reports showing different approaches to defining infrastructure needs and ways to address them, depending on the perspective of the authoring body. However, taken together and interpreted in today's context, all three reports suggest that we should expect lower levels of support for infrastructure and changes in the traditional federal role in financing. Several speakers throughout the day reinforced this idea and offered evidence that a number of options are available, or can be made available, to augment or supplant federal funding.

Dr. Humplick provided the assembly with an international perspective. She discussed nine financing alternatives that have been used throughout the world. These alternatives are not only technically elegant, but they also show how the public and private sectors can balance risk and return. Once the paradigm of public only financing is abandoned, services can be provided in areas where they otherwise would not be. Financing alternatives foster accountability and strengthen links between users and providers in different ways. Dr. Humplick pointed out that the critical factors for success or failure of a project are operating and maintenance costs. During the discussion, she suggested it would be useful if people paid as much attention to infrastructure investments as they do to their private investments.

Ms. Cohen addressed the subject of demographic changes that affect infrastructure financing, including a sobering assessment of the implications of the Orange County, California, bankruptcy. She suggested that money will become increasingly tight as more and more social services are downloaded or devolved from the federal to the state and local level, as happened in the early years of the Reagan administration. The competition for local dollars will continue to increase, as taxpayers, who have greater control over local government, vote their frustrations with government budgets. Local governments concerned with keeping taxes low and containing service costs, partly because of reduced revenues from property taxes, are not likely to invest in infrastructure. The demographic trend toward significantly older property owners, who are traditionally reluctant to support public expenditures for schools and other improvements, provides an interesting counterpoint to the impetus toward intergenerational equity raised earlier by Dr. Brennan. Ms. Cohen noted that there are some bright spots in public spending, high growth areas like North Sioux City, South Dakota, and Rio Rancho, New Mexico, where infrastructure systems are being expanded to keep up with rapid growth. However, some questions were raised about the justification of displacing resources from developed areas to build new infrastructure in areas populated by people who have moved from somewhere else. This is a quasi-philosophical issue, but it shows, in a sense, how wasteful we sometimes are.

The luncheon speaker, Ms. Wince-Smith, pointed out that new technologies represent from 30 to 50 percent of economic growth in an economy like ours and that the infrastructure is a very important element of that. Although we do not have figures showing the percentage of productivity from the infrastructure, she believes this might be useful information for the National Research Council to gather.

The characteristics of a national infrastructure strategy that encourages innovation include the creation of new technologies, which are important to economic growth, and the means of applying them and translating their products into shares in a global marketplace. One suggested method for furthering this scenario was considering vertical, rather than horizontal, partnerships, i.e., users and producers from different industries pooling their resources. The idea is that companies from different industries are more willing to pool resources because they are not in direct competition with each other, and they do not have to worry about antitrust concerns.

In the course of the discussion, the question arose of whether we can compete effectively with the Japanese to develop a sophisticated urban traffic control system, like the one already deployed in Tokyo. Clearly, congestion is a visible problem in cities around the world, a potential market of 200 or more cities in need of traffic control systems.

The afternoon panel, chaired by Dr. Bruce McDowell, discussed the future of infrastructure financing. As director of government policy research for the Advisory Commission on Intergovernmental Relations, Dr. McDowell brings together people from various government agencies to discuss federal infrastructure strategy and ways of financing projects and programs under straitened circumstances. The basic conclusion of the Advisory Commission on Intergovernmental Relations report, "High Performance Public Works," is that financial planning should be included at the very beginning of planning infrastructure projects.

Financial planning is fast becoming a standard part of infrastructure planning. The Intermodal Surface Transportation Efficiency Act (ISTEA) requires that transportation planning at the state and metropolitan levels be done in with financial constraints in mind. Many states and metropolitan planning organizations are hiring financial analysts as part of the planning process. As Dr. McDowell put it, in the past the challenge was to improve public works without new money. Today, we must find ways to improve public works with even less money than we thought we had.

General Charles Williams, with the Greenway toll road project in Virginia, presented another aspect of the infrastructure issue—making money from public works. After his presentation, a question was raised about whether the Greenway project is an individual, isolated case or a project that could serve as a model for other projects. General Williams himself suggested that the Greenway was perhaps not an ideal model, because the cost of equity investment was too high and the public contribution too low—the price for being the first of its kind, he suggested. The project has reached a milestone by opening for operation ahead of schedule.

Ms. Sowder also discussed reasons that the financing of the Greenway will probably not be duplicated. One of many unusual aspects of the financial arrangements for the Greenway is that the owner took on all collateral work associated with development of the road, making it easier for the contractor. What the Greenway can demonstrate, however, and what Ms. Cohen also suggested with some examples from Orange County, is that people are willing to pay user fees to make commuting smoother and faster even if they are not willing to pay higher taxes for government services in general.

In his presentation, Dr. Mudge pointed out that infrastructure has direct benefits, for which people are willing to pay directly, and indirect benefits, such as productivity improvement, which may be greater by an order of magnitude but are difficult to demonstrate, for which people are reluctant to pay. He suggested that "thinking big" is good for the economy, particularly in the case of transportation, because the larger the network the bigger the returns.

In his opinion, however, large networks cannot be financed privately. So the need for public financing remains.

In the 1970s we completed the interstate highway system. In the last 20 years we have been looking for new financing mechanisms because the Highway Trust Fund is past its prime. New public mechanisms, like funds from Section 1012 of the Intermodal Surface Transportation Efficiency Act (ISTEA), have not been applied, however, for a variety of reasons, ranging from lack of imagination to the fact that they are complex and resemble derivatives. According to Dr. Mudge, there is nothing wrong with derivatives, but most people do not understand what they are and that they can be important innovations.

New financing ideas may include infrastructure banks and other institutions or systems that would move us from relying on a single national model, like the Highway Trust Fund, to considering a variety of more flexible models. Dr. Mudge believes, however, that technical innovations have been much greater than financial innovations in the past two years.

Ms. Sowder provided an overview of the private bond market, the primary agency for financing public works. She is optimistic about the strong interest on the part of the investment community in projects with the "right" characteristics, including public support. If there is a benefit, Ms. Sowder said, one probably can charge for it, and so, attract new money.

There are two objectives in infrastructure finance, Ms. Sowder continued. One is using existing funds effectively, and the second is attracting new funds. In terms of using existing funds effectively, Ms. Sowder said, the focus should be on loans rather than grants. Loans not only provide fiscal responsibility, they also replenish themselves. Unlike grants, loans permit recycling of capital. A 3:1 leveraging ratio is appropriate, i.e., borrowing funds amounting to three times the seed money, which may be provided by the federal government.

Mr. Tischler provided some insightful analysis about financial and infrastructure difficulties. Most local jurisdictions do not maintain depreciation accounts as revenue sources for replacing aging or failing infrastructure. He also noted the importance of accounting for operations and maintenance at the time a facility is proposed. Although over the life cycle of a facility these costs far exceed annualized capital costs, they are often ignored until they generate budget shortfalls or tax increases. The solution to this problem lies in better fiscal analysis coupled with public education and communication.

Fiscal analysis can also clarify the levels of service provided by infrastructure. These levels tend to creep up where services have been expanded, increasing the level of expectation without a corresponding increase in financial support. Examples include special education classes, adding required courses, or reducing the number of students per classroom, which translate into higher costs per student in infrastructure support. Unfunded federal mandates, such as bilingual education, are another cause of level of service creep. The financing equation has changed, partly because the public does not understand why infrastructure costs increase while the number of students decreases. Fiscal analysis may provide some solutions to these problems, but communicating results to the public is a major part of the solution.

Mr. Tischler discussed the "cost of urban sprawl" and raised a very important, but counterintuitive, point that is often missed. Although infrastructure costs tend to be higher for lower density development, the tax revenue from higher value, low density housing can more than offset the higher cost of infrastructure.

In the ensuing discussion, Dr. Humplick suggested that financing transportation infrastructure will remain in the public sector, the Greenway notwithstanding, but other infrastructure projects are likely to be privately financed. In any case, we need a new, more flexible financing model for transportation projects. Ray Sterling noted that the public may be reluctant to support projects where resources, particularly resources like water, are allocated to private, rather than public, utilities. Mr. Tischler concluded by suggesting that solutions are available, some of them quite simple. But they will not work unless there is public confidence in government. If people do not fully understand the issues, they tend to mistrust the government and are reluctant to support necessary projects and associated fiscal solutions.

Balancing Present Costs and Future Benefits

Timothy J. Brennan
University of Maryland, Baltimore County
Resources for the Future

I have been asked to talk about policy issues associated with finance, some of which may be connected to ethical issues involving what we do now for future generations. First, I need to set the stage by establishing some principles for thinking about the financing of infrastructure projects in particular and public budgeting and deficits in general.

There are important differences between public and private finance in how one might balance present costs and future benefits. A key distinction, certainly with regard to policy decisions, is the distinction between "resource flows" (the actual movements of goods and services) and "money flows" (issues of how and by whom payments are made). Understanding this distinction has important implications for how we interpret budget deficits. As we will see, confusion between resource flows and money flows affects public opinion regarding deficits and decisions about which infrastructure investments are worth making and which are not.

After discussing resource flows and money flows, I want to talk about future generations and the discount rates we use to evaluate infrastructure investments. Before doing so, some definitions may be in order. The idea of discounting future benefits with respect to present costs means, simply, that we require that every dollar of present investment has to generate more than a dollar in future benefits before we decide to invest it. The discount rate, like an interest rate, is a way of measuring how much future benefits should be discounted annually before we can see if they are great enough to warrant present investment. For example, if a one-dollar investment today has to generate two dollars in benefits 10 years from now, we would say that the discount rate applied to that investment is about 7 percent. This, not coincidentally, is the amount that a one-dollar investment has to earn per year to be worth two dollars 10 years from now.

The questions raised by discounting are numerous and highly controversial. Should we use discount rates from private financial markets to tell public policymakers how much the interests of future generations should count? We will see that it is at least questionable whether what we actually do in markets tells us what we should do in policy settings.

To understand how to approach the issue, we will look at a couple of potentially conflicting views on whether, in making investment decisions, we discount the interests of future generations or not. The "opportunity cost" way of looking at investments insists that we compare infrastructure investments to what we could have earned in the future if we had put the money elsewhere. The "equal standing" approach denies that interests should be treated preferentially just because they happen to belong to present individuals rather than individuals living in the future. After examining and comparing these approaches to evaluating infrastructure investments, I will turn to ethical (as opposed to narrowly economic) arguments for why we might want to discount benefits to future generations when deciding which infrastructure investments are worth making and which are not.

PUBLIC POLICY TOWARD PRIVATE
INFRASTRUCTURE INVESTMENTS

What makes financing a policy issue? I assume we are not worried here about evaluating privately financed investments. What General Motors decides to do with money in building factories is up to the company because GM reaps the benefits and GM bears the costs. Applying principles of private financing may not be enough to arrive at the right decisions, however, when there are different kinds of market failures.

One such context involves monopolies. Experience with infrastructure investments in the telecommunications and electric utility industries indicates that the absence of competition or the regulatory mechanisms we have put in place to replace competition may lead firms to invest too little or too much. Public policies involving government mandates, public financing, or subsidy programs may be necessary to ensure that monopolies do not withhold investments in order to keep supplies low and prices high or overinvest to exploit regulatory commitments to cover costs.

A second category of market failure warranting public concern with private investments involves what economists call "externalities." These arise when private investments generate costs and benefits that accrue to third parties beyond their markets. Businesses will be less willing to invest in infrastructure or anything else if they cannot capitalize on costs and benefits by charging whoever benefits. If benefits cannot be captured in markets, the public may have to make the investment. This principle applies not just to physical infrastructures; it is the primary argument for public funding of basic scientific research that is not protected by patents and copyrights.

A third source of public concern with private investments is "asymmetric information." There may be situations where someone who is thinking about undertaking an infrastructure investment knows something that buyers on the other side of the market do not, or vice versa. This can cause markets to fall apart because the buyers without the crucial information stay away to avoid being exploited by buyers who have it. Asymmetric information is a very important concern in health insurance—which, in the eyes of some, is as much a part of the nation's infrastructure as highways, power lines, and telephone networks.

PUBLIC PROJECTS: RESOURCE FLOWS AND MONEY FLOWS

Although market failures are important—but not sufficient— conditions for justifying public intervention, my main purpose is to talk about issues posed by public financing, either through state or federal governments. There are two questions here that are inseparable. One is the decision to spend in the first place. Do we take public resources and use them to create, expand, or augment the infrastructure in some way? The second question is how we fund this spending. Do we tax? Do we borrow? Do we rely on user fees, if that option is available and feasible?

The main point is that resource flows, not money flows, are what matter. The real cost of the infrastructure is not money we take away from the future but resources not devoted to consumption or to building things today. If our choice is, say, between installing fiber-optic networks and expanding hospitals, then the cost of doing the former is that we strip resources from the latter. This is an example of what economists call "opportunity cost."

This sort of choice arises whether the funding comes through borrowing, taxation, or some other source. But if resource flows are what matter, then what is the importance, if any, of budget deficits, i.e., financing public expenditures via borrowing rather than taxation? This is a money flow rather than a resource flow question. We should look at some arguments about why budget deficits, as a money flow issue, may not matter very much and then turn to some responses to those arguments.

BORROWING FROM OURSELVES

The first thing to notice is that public budget deficits have no direct effect on resource flow. One cannot move production and resources from the future to the present simply by changing how one finances things. The idea that when we run deficits we are somehow robbing the future to pay for the present, therefore, cannot be right, at least not in simple terms. Quite literally, the future is not here for us to rob now! If 25 or 50 years from now, someone's labor is going to go into building a car, we cannot take that car, hence that labor, from the future and put it into the present to be used today. There may be implications for the future from our present investment decisions and perhaps from our financing decisions, but it is impossible to take wealth yet to be generated and transfer it, as if by time machine, into the present.

If financing has an effect on resource flows, it has to be fairly subtle. Deficit-financed infrastructure does not come from future taxpayers but from reduced consumption or reduced alternative investment from present bondholders. To be sure, future taxpayers will end up with fewer resources—i.e., poorer—to pay off the debt. But those payments do not go to us in the present. They go to other people in the future who hold the government bonds that are being paid off.

This is basically a long way of restating the familiar argument that deficits are not important because we "owe the money to ourselves." For every future dollar paid by taxpayers because of deficit financing, a dollar will be paid to a bondholder. One could as easily say that deficit financing creates a windfall for some future persons (the bondholders), as we frequently say that such financing robs other future persons (the taxpayers). By paying attention to how dollars are moved around, we can see that deficit financing does not move resources from future taxpayers to present consumers.

A somewhat more sophisticated way of viewing this is what economists call the "Ricardian Equivalence Theorem." On that account, deficit financing does not matter because, if the government borrows now, it creates a future tax liability because of the need to pay off the bondholders from which it borrowed. If governments and individuals can borrow at the same rate, people will view that future tax liability as a financial burden equivalent to what they would have borne if they paid taxes today rather than let the government borrow. In that sense, deficits do not matter. This is the public finance analog to the "Modigliani-Miller Theorem" in corporate finance, which says that financing private capital through debt or equity does not matter because it ends up having no effect on the individuals who end up putting up the money. If the company itself does not borrow, individuals could borrow to finance stock purchases.

Returning to the government deficit context, if we were to eliminate the budget deficit tomorrow by raising taxes, people could borrow to pay their taxes and maintain current consumption levels. From the point of view of the bondholder and the macroeconomy, it would not make any difference whether the government or individuals issued the bonds. In fact, if there would be a market where some want to borrow and some want to lend, and if the government has capital market advantages that other borrowers lack, it is probably better for the government than for individuals to run a deficit. This is an example of the degree of detail necessary to come up with a real effect of money flows.

WHY FINANCING MATTERS

Like a lot of arguments in economics, the "borrowing from ourselves" and Ricardian Equivalence arguments are caricatures. Nonetheless, they show that money flows may not be very important compared to resource flows. However, there is a lot of concern regarding financing, and some of it is justified. Let me take a brief look at some of the criticisms of these caricatures.

Importing Investment Capital

A first reason why financing might matter to us as a nation is that the resource flows may not be just among ourselves. They may be coming from or going to someplace else, and we may care about that. Resources used to build the infrastructure today may be coming from foreign investors willing to defer consumption now in exchange for greater consumption later. By borrowing in this way, we are obliging future U.S. taxpayers to send resources abroad. In this sense, we do not simply owe ourselves.

This is obviously a major concern among state project financiers, who have no reason to think bonds are going to be held by people who live in state. (This may explain why many states have balanced budget laws, while the federal government does not.) On the other side of the coin, perhaps we should be more ethical or broad-minded about the issue. Is it merely parochial to care if we deprive future U.S. taxpayers and benefit foreign bondholders?

Tax Avoidance Strategies

A second reason why financing might matter involves economic distortions associated with collecting taxes. Moving money around is not as simple as it may look. There are real economic costs to redistributing purchasing power, including shifting purchasing power from taxpayers to bondholders. If we have to raise taxes in the future to raise the funds to pay off bondholders, people will start doing things to avoid paying those taxes—working less, investing less, looking for shelters.

These avoidance tactics make the economy less productive. If, because of a deficit, we are going to have to raise future taxes to pay off future bondholders, there will be deleterious effects in the future. Of course, if the alternative is financing by increasing taxes now, we will create similar effects in the present. Ascertaining which is worse or when these effects balance involves subtle, complex estimates of discount rates and marginal tax burdens.

Shifting Productivity to Present

A third point is that if you know taxes are going to go up in the future because of debt financing, you might have an incentive to work harder now and avoid working later or to consume now rather than invest, shifting income to the present to avoid paying future taxes. You would be reallocating your effort to generating wealth in the present rather than in the future. This reduces savings, the rate of resource accumulation, and bequests to future generations.

I do not know how large the effect of the shift is. An interesting aspect of it is that one argument against the idea (from the "Ricardian Equivalence Theorem") that future tax payments create a present liability is that people are too myopic to think that way. However, they must be farsighted to engage in income-shifting behavior. Thus, these two criticisms rely on contradictory assumptions.

Lax Fiscal Discipline

The myopia argument brings us to the last, and perhaps most important, point about the importance of financing related to fiscal discipline. This may be what underlies a lot of concern with and opposition to the deficit. The goal of many deficit opponents is to reduce excessive government spending by limiting borrowing. Their premise is that control over money flows (bondholders to taxpayers today, taxpayers to bondholders tomorrow) would control resource flows (public investment rather than private investment or consumption). The underlying idea might be that in a democracy, a myopic or present-oriented majority might believe that they are getting something for nothing when the government borrows. If so, this creates a bias toward public investment and away from private investment, which may not be in our economic interest.

SHOULD WE BUILD AND FOR WHOM?

Whether these financing effects are major first-order effects or minor second-order effects is something about which economists argue a great deal. The answer is likely to vary from context to context. The reason I offer this short review on the basic economics of deficit spending is to indicate why I believe financial issues are second order. Ultimately, we should be talking more about whether or not an investment should be made and not so much about how it should be financed—recognizing, of course, that it should be financed as efficiently as possible.

This brings us to the generational issue. The decision to make a public investment in infrastructure is a decision to direct resources away from current consumption and private investments to benefit people in the future. The first-order question is whether or not to build. Do we construct new highways? Do we expand the water system? Do we invest hundreds of billions of dollars in a fiber-optic broadband telecommunications network? These concerns are similar to concerns that arise when considering investing in ecological conservation and environmental protection.

One might break the to-build-or-not-to-build question down by looking first at whether we are talking about shorter term investments for shorter term payoffs. To borrow an observation from Professor Thomas Schelling of the University of Maryland, decisions about investments with benefits that fall within our lifetimes are essentially decisions we make for ourselves and do not raise a profound ethical or policy issue involving future generations. If the payoffs come in 5, 10, or 20 years, we can say with some confidence that we do not have to worry about whether we are properly taking into account the interests of future generations in the cost-benefit calculation.

Investments in infrastructure or the environment that will last for decades raise harder, long-term generational issues. In telecommunications, for example, there are significant questions about whether or not to build a fiber-optic infrastructure that could be in place for half a century. Nuclear power plant construction and waste disposal effects may span centuries. Debates over reducing industrial growth to lessen the "greenhouse effect" or to protect endangered species raise deep concerns about whether markets reflect the interests of future generations in terms of resource conservation and environmental protection.

How should we take the interests of future generations into account in making these decisions? Should we do what markets tell us to do in terms of how future benefits translate into money and how much future money is worth today, after discounting? Should we discount future benefits at all? These questions, which are already difficult, become even more difficult because of the uncertainty about the future benefits of ecological policies. In the eyes of many, that uncertainty colors the decision about how much we should take future interests into account.

DISCOUNTING

Sound policymaking requires that we review our tools for deciding if capital market discount rates should measure if long-term future benefits are worth present costs. There is a great deal of controversy about how discount rates figure in cost-benefit tests. Some of the controversy, I believe, rests on conceptual confusion. To understand that confusion and, I hope, to get past it, we should focus on one particular factor that goes into the determination of market discount rates—"pure time preference."

We can look at what determines market discount rates in a very general sense. Many of you know more about the specific determinants than I, but a simple, gut-level analysis can make the point. On the demand side, the level of economic activity affects how much entrepreneurs and corporate managers are willing to borrow at given interest rates. In terms of the cost of supplying capital, you have to compensate people for expected inflation and for risk.

Most important for the generational policy question, markets compensate those who supply capital for what economists call "pure time preference," a term that refers to how much people have to be paid in added future consumption to get them to defer the chance to consume now. In other words, how much do you have to be paid for deferral, over and above compensation for inflationary declines in the value of money and for the risk that you may not get your principal back?

The pure time preference part of the discount rate raises the most serious ethical questions. Accepting market-based discount rates as the standard for weighing future benefits against present costs implies accepting whatever pure time preferences we happen to have—how we choose the present over the future in our private saving and investment decisions—as appropriate. Accordingly, this leads us to the opportunity cost standard for evaluating infrastructure investments by requiring that investments produce a stream of benefits at least as great as could be obtained by taking those funds and investing them elsewhere, e.g., in the stock market.

The problem with holding future benefits to an opportunity cost standard is that it can trivialize them over the very long term. At a 6 percent discount rate, it takes a $340 return one hundred years from now to be worth a dollar today. If investing that dollar paid only $339, it wouldn't be worth it. To take a fairly well known example, it does not take a large discount rate for the $24 paid for Manhattan Island in the early seventeenth century to have been a good deal for the Indians. At 6 percent, that investment would be worth about $40 billion today, a figure comparable to the aggregate earnings of the current residents in Manhattan.

We do need to remember that market interest rates include more than pure time preference. They also reflect inflationary expectations and compensation for bearing risks, neither of which is particularly problematic. The 6 percent figure chosen here is rigged on the high side, perhaps by quite a bit. Many estimates of the pure time preference component of the interest rate are lower, some as low as 2 percent. If the interest rate is 3 percent, the hundred-year rate of return ratio falls from 340 to 1 to only 19 to 1. Still, at 19 to 1, it would not appear that we are treating benefits a hundred years from now equally in an ethically acceptable sense of evaluating infrastructure investments.

EQUAL STANDING: ADDING ETHICS TO ECONOMICS

The 19 to 1 ratio remains a rather gross violation of what, from a legal or philosophical perspective, we might think of as an "equal standing" principle. Why should present generations get to count 19 (or 340) times as much as generations a hundred years hence? The conflict between equal standing and opportunity cost principles, because both are plausible, is undeniable.

Public finance textbooks contain a variety of attempts to rig market rates to conform better to ethical viewpoints. For example, a great deal of attention is devoted to whether we should use pre-tax market rates or post-tax returns as measures of the discount rate. There is not enough time to delve into the fine points of this discussion except to observe that it is born, in part, out of the hope of finding an opportunity cost measure more in line with equal standing principles.

I think this hope is misbegotten because it tries to force a round, descriptive economic concept into a square, ethical hole. The confusion arises because too little attention is paid to methodology. One has to separate the normative question, "should we assist future generations," from the empirical question, "if yes, than how." Philosophers refer to this kind of error as a "category mistake."

Empirical and normative issues belong in two different categories. In the eighteenth century, British philosopher David Hume propounded the idea that what "is" does not imply what "ought" to be. Despite how something is, we need to come up with an independent ethical justification before we conclude that this "is" tells us what we ought to do. Merely looking at how something is currently done does not solve the problem. I am suggesting that when it comes to infrastructure investments, the opportunity costs are important, but they are only the "is" part of the story. They do not necessarily play a role in deciding the "ought" question. It is important to keep these concepts separate.

An example may clarify why markets do not tell us what to do regarding future generations and why we need an ethical premise of some kind to get at the question. The example is unrealistic, but its extreme nature makes the difference between the "is" and the "ought" easy to remember. Assume for the moment that generations of people do not overlap. Everyone lives for 75 years, and then they all die at once. Out of the ground comes the next generation of people, like tulips. Assume also that there are no cross-generational connections or families, i.e., that no one today knows that a particular person 75 years in the future happens to be a "descendant" in some genetic or functional way.

Let us suppose one generation of these tulip-people faces an issue of long-term infrastructure investment, e.g., whether or not to build an elaborate highway system that will last into the next generation—the members of which the present generation will never know, see, or experience in any specific way. One might expect that the present generation would forego the investment and consume very quickly. Beyond their own lifetimes, the discount rate would be infinite—subsequent generations would count for naught. Future persons would simply not matter.

Even in this setting, I think it would be hard to argue that future generations "ought" to have no claim on present resources, despite the fact that the discount rate "is" infinite. The tulip-people's attitudes that future tulip-people do not count does not mean they ought not count. In our own world, our ethical obligations and duties to make investments or conserve resources for the future are not just by-products of the happenstance that generations really do overlap. The tulip-people example illustrates how there can be a difference between what markets tell us to do and the right thing to do. We cannot decide if future benefits of infrastructure investment or environmental protection are worth present costs simply by looking at market rates of return.

The distinction between opportunity cost market measures of investment worth and equal standing appraisals would not matter if investments that ranked higher on one scale necessarily ranked higher on the other. This issue would lose most of its force if investments earned a higher rate of return if and only if they yielded more benefits overall, counting future recipients equal to present recipients. Unfortunately, things do not work that way.

Consider two investments. One involves giving up $100 billion today in consumption benefits to put in a high-speed communications network that will last for 20 years. A second involves putting that $100 billion sacrifice into new technologies that produce less carbon dioxide, leading to a meaningful reduction of mean global temperatures, but only after 100 years. The first investment may pass an opportunity cost test, while the second one fails, at prevailing market rates. However, if benefits in 20 years and benefits in 100 years are given equal weight, the carbon dioxide abatement investment might win out over the communications network.

ETHICAL JUSTIFICATIONS FOR DISCOUNTING

The contrast so far between the economic and ethical perspectives on discounting is extreme, largely because a meaningful discount rate eventually means that, at some point, future generations count for very little in current policy calculations. However, the discipline of ethics is not quite so simple. There are some philosophical appeals one could make to support some degree of discounting.

Some of these appeals hinge on future generations being much wealthier than the present generation. A number of economists expect future generations to be wealthier, in keeping with historical trends up to the present, because of the greater knowledge that will be available to them. There is speculation on the other side as well, focusing on material resource constraints.

If future generations are wealthier, then there is a justification for discounting, according to Professor (and recent Nobel Prize winner) John Harsanyi of the University of California. He offers an ethical theory grounded in the obligation to maximize aggregate utility over time. This framework can support discounting. If people in the future will be wealthier than we are today, a dollar will give them less utility than we get from that dollar. To compensate, we should not give up dollars unless they produce more dollars for them, i.e., we should apply a positive discount rate. Conversely, if one believes that people in the future will be poorer than we are today, a dollar to them is already worth more than a dollar is worth to us. In that case, a negative discount rate would apply, i.e., we should invest on their behalf even if they get less in dollars than we give up.

A different and more stark perspective comes from Harvard philosopher John Rawls. His "theory of justice" is derived from a hypothetical scenario in which persons collectively decide, behind a "veil of ignorance," how resources should be allocated over time. The linchpin of his argument is that the individuals making allocations do not know in advance in which generation they will live. Rawls contends that if people do not know where they will end up, they will be averse to risk. Consequently, they will adopt a "maximin" rule to maximize the welfare of the generation least well off.

According to the "maximin" rule, we would always adopt investment policies that would make poorer generations better off, regardless of the sacrifice from other generations. If future generations are expected to be poorer than we are, sacrifices may be warranted even if the gains to them are far outweighed by the losses to us. If they are richer, however, we need not give their interests any weight, i.e., we could justifiably adopt an infinite discount rate.

A third approach, recognizing perspectives from feminist philosophy, is offered by philosophers Susan Wolf and Martha Nussbaum, who point out that equal standing, however noble in theory, is extreme in practice. Equal standing denies fundamental aspects of what it means to be a person. It is an integral part of our humanity to put our families and friends ahead of strangers. We may put our nation ahead of other nations. We may put generations we know—our children and grandchildren—ahead of generations far enough in the future to be strangers. To deny ourselves the moral right to favor some generations over others undercuts the validity of the specific connections that form our lives, and would turn us into rationalizing machines instead of people.

FINAL WORD TO THE PRESENT

I would like to close with another observation from Professor Schelling. In talking about discounting, he has noted that we worry a great deal about what we should do for people in the future, but, in the meantime, we do not seem to be worrying nearly as much about poor people in the world today. The conclusion I draw is that we ought to think about our current spatial discount factors—how much we count benefits to people elsewhere in the world, elsewhere in our country, elsewhere in our communities—as opposed to worrying about the huge ethical problem of comparing claims over time. The debate about how to judge the benefits of future infrastructure investment against present costs is important, but it ought not to keep us from recognizing serious problems in the here and now that we should, perhaps, invest in solving as well.

DISCUSSION

Dr. Bugliarello: This last example from Professor Schelling shows the drift from economics to philosophy because it is basically philosophical. In many cases infrastructure is planned and built with the expectation that demand will increase over time. How does that play into the setting of discounting and ethical considerations?

Dr. Brennan: Off the top of my head, that would play in a couple of ways. One, if you think the reason demand is increasing over time is because economies are developing over time, that is an argument for positive discounting because it shows that people will be wealthier. On the other hand, if you think the reason demand for infrastructure is increasing over time is that alternatives are becoming more expensive, then people will be effectively less wealthy without the investment, arguing for a lower discount rate. In either case, an equal standing or an opportunity cost perspective is obviously going to tilt the balance in favor of making the future investment.

The mystery about a lot of investments I am familiar with, particularly telecommunications, is that they are so speculative it is hard to know what the costs and benefits will be. This is the fiber-optic argument. I remember a year or so ago hearing a talk endorsing spending the hundreds of billions it would take to put in a fiber-optic telecommunications infrastructure. The speaker, Henry Geller, quite self-consciously gave the field of dreams argument for it, "If you build it, they will come."

At lease Henry was honest, and I give him credit for that. Some people make grand claims about what people are going to do when, in fact, they do not know. He said, "Look, I don't know what they are going to do, but I think it is worth building anyhow." How you defend that judgment to the taxpayers, rate payers, or whoever is picking up the tab, I am not exactly sure, but I admire his candor.

Participant: We all assume that in the future telecommunications will have a significant impact on the way we live and where we live, which in turn may have some impact on the kind of support infrastructure we need to provide for the future population. Do you have any observations on the economics of that scenario?

Dr. Brennan: I do not have any profound factual observations, but there are two arguments, one inside and one outside economics, that deal with it. The one within economics is that it is like boosting demand, and if you happen to have information to make judgments about the costs, you can at least conceptualize it.

The harder argument is that economic arguments and, to a large extent, philosophical arguments take people as a given. When that assumption is not true, economic arguments fall apart because things are judged against the demands of people. If you think something is going to change, not just in the sense of being more valuable but actually changing what people want and, in a very real sense, who they are, as economists define identity, then you are trying to measure benefits and costs with an elastic yard-stick. You have to look outside economics to make those kinds of judgments.

What do you do if a decision affects who people are, their numbers, and so on? Are we better off in a world with fewer people who are wealthier, on average, or more people, who are poorer? The frameworks we are most comfortable with talk about fixed sets of people. When we're dealing with things that have effects on population patterns, for example, fundamental questions or conceptions we use to address them do not seem to work very well.

How would you evaluate building an infrastructure one way if it means one set of people is going to be alive and reap the benefits and that they would not be the same people who would exist if we built it another way? As a result of infrastructures, people move, people meet each other, people are born. In what sense would we be depriving one set of people who are not very well off by building one way when they might not be around at all if we built another way? How do we make those kinds of comparisons? I could go into some of the very thorny examples and paradoxes philosophers have identified in thinking about these questions, but it would not really tell you a whole lot about how to solve these puzzles.

Participant: How would changing governmental accounting affect this argument?

Dr. Brennan: Do you mean whether or not we count capital expenditure as part of the deficit? I do not think it would affect my overall argument, other than in the indirect feedback effects on resource flows, primarily through fiscal discipline. If you think that, for a variety of reasons, it would make sense to have fairly substantial budget deficits or that we should not shrink them very much, then changing to an accounting system where deficits are viewed as less threatening than they are now, by and large, would be a good idea. I am not sure that it has a direct real effect, however, because the important factors are not money flows but resource flows. To get a real effect, you have to trace the accounting effect to a resource flow. The main response I want to leave you with is that accounting practice is not likely to have an instantaneous, simple, breakthrough effect on infrastructure investment and budgeting policy.

Infrastructure Challenges and Issues: A Panel

Nancy Connery, moderator
Consultant, Public Infrastructure

At this juncture, I think it is important to rethink the issue of the infrastructure. It is clearly not at the apex of public attention and policy. It had its day perhaps, and it may yet have another, but right now it is in a quiet phase. I have looked at this phase with some despair at times because I know all of us have worked hard to make public works issues a much more important aspect of public policy. But we know that the facilities and their problems are not going to go away. So, to the extent that we can, this is a good time to take stock.

The issue has become much more textured, I think, since we started 10 or 15 years ago counting up the wish list of things we would like to do or think we should do. It now has many ramifications, some of which were just brought home to us by Dr. Brennan. Our three panelists will provide insights on the challenges and issues in infrastructure finance that lie ahead. Although domestic and international infrastructure requirements differ in both type and degree, the relationship between a healthy infrastructure and economic vitality is universal.

Domestic Agenda

Carol Everett
Rebuild America Coalition

It is interesting that although the issue of infrastructure investment is on the political back burner right now, a proliferation of new reports is coming out on the subject. I have selected three of these reports to talk about today, reports that offer very different perspectives on the topic but all of which are important to a full appreciation of the dimensions of the issue. I will describe each report quickly, make a few comments, and then offer some final remarks on where we need to go from here.

The first report is a congressional report that was released this past January (1995) by the House Committee on Public Works and Transportation (recently renamed the House Committee on Transportation and Infrastructure). This report is entitled simply "National Transportation and Environmental Infrastructure Needs" and takes a fairly traditional approach. The second report was also released in January 1995, "The Case for Public Investment" prepared by the Economic Policy Institute (EPI), a Washington, D.C., think tank. This report takes a macroeconomic modeling approach to the issue of whether our nation should be investing more in infrastructure. The third report was prepared by the U.S. Army Corps of Engineers. It is called "Living Within Constraints: An Emerging Vision for High Performance Public Works" and incorporates viewpoints from all of the major interest groups concerned with our nation's infrastructure.

The three reports are a good follow up to Dr. Brennan's remarks because they bring into high relief the whole question of what we "ought" to be doing as a nation versus what we "can" do. One of my theories after studying these three reports is that where you come out on the infrastructure investment issue has more to do with your initial assumptions about the flexibility of the federal government to solve these problems than about almost anything else.

HOUSE OF REPRESENTATIVES REPORT

Let me turn first to the House report. To produce this report, the House public works committee used data from industry and government experts and anecdotal from that can be described for the most part as physical or engineering analysis. Based upon this information, the House concluded that "there is a chronic underinvestment in the nation's infrastructure that is threatening our national economy and living standards." The report examines various categories of infrastructure.

Major portions of our national highway system are in substandard condition, severely impeding and inhibiting the economic growth and mobility that have been hallmarks of this system. Almost one-fourth of our highways are in poor or mediocre condition; another 36 percent are rated fair. One in five of the nation's bridges is structurally deficient, meaning weight restrictions have been set to limit truck traffic.

The nation's transit infrastructure has suffered greatly from a prolonged period of underinvestment that has curtailed service, reduced ridership, threatened the existence of many transit systems, and left substantial needs unmet. Almost one-fourth of the rail transit facilities are in poor condition, and one-fifth of the transit buses must be replaced as soon as possible. In virtually all areas, service levels are inadequate, reducing the mobility of millions of people who depend on public transit.

The nation's airport and airway system is steadily becoming more congested. Growth in passenger and air cargo traffic since deregulation in 1978 has been explosive. Passenger traffic is expected to double almost in the next decade, and cargo traffic is growing even faster. Currently, there are unacceptable flight delays at 23 of the nation's major airports. If no improvements are made, 33 major airports will have unacceptable delays by the year 2002.

The nation's deep-draft shipping ports, which handle 95 percent of our international trade, face severe access problems on both water-side and land-side. Major ports on all of our coasts have been confronted with serious delays in obtaining dredging permits and other necessary approvals. At the same time, land-side connections have often been ignored because they are not part of a well defined transportation program. As a result, shipments to and from ports face inordinate delays and congestion, often increasing shipping costs.

The nation's inland waterways have outdated and antiquated locks and dams that hinder the movement of coal, grain, and other bulk products. Delays in passing through these locks can cause significant increases in shipping costs. In 1990, 10 locks on the inland waterway system averaged more than three hours of delay per barge tow; while many other locks caused lesser delays. With use of the inland waterway system expected to increase each year, delays are likely to increase. Fully 40 percent of the nation's locks are more than half a century old, and one lock on the Kentucky River is 150 years old. Nearly 90 percent of our locks and dams are too small to handle modern barge tows.

Our drinking water systems are also deteriorating. Many are using water pipes 100 years old or more. These outdated systems may spring leaks and are subject to widespread contamination. Contaminated water has caused 900 deaths and causes almost one million illnesses every year. In a two-year period, violations of federal drinking water standards were reported in 43 percent of the nation's drinking water systems, which supply water for 43 million people.

Our wastewater treatment infrastructure remains inadequate to the task of cleaning up the nation's waters. A third or more of our rivers, lakes, ponds, reservoirs, and estuaries remain polluted, as does almost the entire Great Lakes shoreline. Sewage treatment needs are especially urgent for metropolitan areas trying to remedy the problem of combined sewer overflows and small communities lacking independent financing ability.

I know some people in this audience are critical of the needs approach used by the House because, for the most part, it doesn't look at how systems are performing from an outcomes perspective. But I believe at this moment this is the best we can do to provide an overall picture of our nation's infrastructure. And for that reason the House report is invaluable.

Okay, so what does the House report conclude? First, national leaders must develop a strategy for meeting our vast transportation and environmental infrastructure needs, establish priorities with the greatest economic and environmental returns, and develop sources of funding. (The report covers a host of financing options but does not come out in favor of one set of strategies or another.)

Second, the House report concludes that the infrastructure issue must be elevated to the high level of public visibility that it deserves. (How to do this is something the Rebuild America Coalition has been struggling with for the past eight years.) The House committee believes that higher visibility will help develop a broad national consensus on infrastructure issues and that this consensus can be a springboard for action.

Finally, the House report supports establishing a federal capital budget and taking the highway, airport, and waterways trust funds off budget.

ECONOMIC POLICY INSTITUTE REPORT

In the second report, the Economic Policy Institute (EPI) takes a very different approach from the House public works committee. EPI is interested in spurring the growth rate of family incomes in our country. EPI starts off by saying that "for a quarter of a century following World War II, American families could count on rising living standards propelled by rising real wages. But over the last two decades family incomes have grown hardly at all, and what growth there has been has been a result of more workers per family, not higher wages." EPI asserts that to reverse this slide and ensure a healthy future for America's standard of living, we need to become more productive. The key to boosting productivity is investment, both private and public.

To support this thesis, EPI compares infrastructure investment in industrialized nations and finds that the U.S. ranks dead last in terms of infrastructure investment as a percentage of GDP. In 1992, for example, Japan invested roughly three times as much as the U.S. Moreover, EPI says that the value of America's stock of public infrastructure has been decreasing. During the 1960s and 1970s the public infrastructure stock grew steadily, according to EPI, but over the past decade it has fallen without interruption from nearly 55 percent of GDP in 1982 to less than 40 percent in 1992.

The EPI report concludes that, "however one measures it, the U.S. is not investing enough in public infrastructure and that we are paying a high price for this practice in terms of declining incomes and opportunities." It goes on to say that "if we do not reverse this trend the price will only rise. We owe much of today's living standards to yesterday's citizens who believed they had a shared obligation to invest in America's future. It is our obligation to our own future and to those who come after us to replenish our nation's capital stock."

U.S. ARMY CORPS OF ENGINEERS REPORT

The last report I want to discuss was prepared by the U.S. Army Corps of Engineers. The publication date says January 1995, but I believe it was released to the public in September. This report wraps up a three year effort to define a new federal strategy as a component of a broader national strategy aimed at bringing federal programs into better alignment with state, local and private sector needs. It builds on the fine work of the National Council on Public Works Improvement.

This is an excellent report and very comprehensive in terms of coverage of the infrastructure topic. My remarks today cannot in any way do justice to its breadth and depth. Because I am running out of time, I am only going to talk about how it approaches the issue of whether America should be investing more in public works infrastructure.

In my opinion, this report seems to say that the nation's financial resources are so constrained that it is not productive to discuss what the optimal level of infrastructure investment should be. Yes, the report says, "public infrastructure investment does matter to economic growth and productivity," but because in reality "there is little, if any, new funding available for increased public works spending anyway," we have "moved beyond arguments over whether America is truly underinvesting in public works, or whether public investment really matters to the economy."

Following this line of thought, the report concludes with recommendations for maintaining what we have better, focusing on demand management and low cost solutions. This report sees a much reduced financial role for the federal government than the first two reports do.

CONCLUSION

Getting back to the theory I presented at the beginning of my talk, I believe the world views described in these three reports are natural extensions of the organizations they represent. For example, EPI's focus on a federal solution is logical for an organization whose mission is to think broadly about national economic problems but has no implementing authority. I also find it reasonable that the House recommends a more conservative federal role than in the past now that Congress is arguing over a smaller and smaller discretionary budget and feels increasingly powerless faced with a budget deficit problem of seemingly insurmountable proportions. The Corps, on the other hand, is a federal agency. I am only guessing here, but I expect the range of solutions that it can envision is somewhat restricted by what is currently acceptable to the administration. It would, therefore, make sense that the Corps sees the nation's options as pretty constrained right now—more constrained than EPI or Congress.

So, where should we go from here? In my opinion, all of these world views are important to understanding the full complexity of the infrastructure investment question and need to be carried forward into an effort to achieve a consensus on a national infrastructure investment strategy. And how should we go about developing a consensus on a national infrastructure investment strategy? A first step would be to update the National Council on Public Works Improvement report card, which rated America's infrastructure performance in "Fragile Foundations." This will be a difficult undertaking, if it is to be done right, but we need a way of communicating to the American public how this nation is doing in terms of moving people and goods, disposing of our wastes, and providing safe drinking water. "Doing this right" will mean utilizing the path-breaking research findings of the National Research Council on measuring and improving infrastructure performance.

After that, I think we need to convene a national conference that brings together all of the players at the national, state, and local levels, including the private sector. Everyone seems to know that the rules are changing in Washington, but what the new rules mean for the different players in the infrastructure delivery partnership are not clear. I believe a conference would do a great deal to clarify roles and provide guidance on how to sift through the various infrastructure financing options.

International Perspective

Frannie Humplick
World Bank

The information I will be reporting on comes from a World Bank report that came out last year. Assuming that the public sector will be limited in its ability to finance infrastructure in the future and that, therefore, we have to look at alternatives outside the public sector, I will not look at government infrastructure funds or municipal funds because those are still options in public investment.

In terms of scale, developing countries at present are spending about $200 billion a year as a group on infrastructure. About 90 percent of that investment is financed by the public sector, either through tax revenues or by borrowing in ways that the public sector mediates. What is interesting is that infrastructure investment in developing countries is a large fraction of public investment and also of total investment. The share of infrastructure as part of total investment is between 20 and 30 percent, depending on whether the country is a low-income or a middle-income country. As a share of public investments, the percentage is even higher—more than 30 percent and, in some cases, up to 60 percent.

This is an interesting trend because, with two exceptions, in developing countries infrastructure investments have been continuously privatized. The exceptions are road infrastructure, which has largely remained in the public sector, and power generation in countries with limited energy resources where most generation and transmission have remained in the public sector. Water supply and other areas of infrastructure have been provided by lower levels of government and, in some cases, the private sector. Public investment in infrastructure covers mostly road and energy infrastructure.

The infrastructure problem, internationally as well as domestically, has a number of characteristics. The first one is maintenance. When we talk about infrastructure, $200 billion a year is invested in new capital or the major rehabilitation of existing capital. Not usually included are expenditures on maintenance or operating costs, which come under the current budget. To show you what the scale of the problem is, I will use a ratio developed by the International Monetary Fund from our projects around the world for macroeconomic and planning purposes. The ratio is called the "r coefficient," which is the ratio of maintenance and operating expenditures to initial investment of capital expenditures annualized.

Depending on the type of infrastructure, there is a huge change in the importance of capital versus recurrent expenditures. So when we talk about financing, it is important to distinguish between financing of the initial, major works and annually recurring expenditures. Some categories of expenditures have a higher ratio of recurrence to capital investments. These include buildings in education and health and, within the category of roads, feeder roads, which are more maintenance intensive than higher technology roads like paved roads and state roads in general.

The second issue is that foreign financing is an important component of the infrastructure investment problem. At present, about 12 percent, $24 billion a year, is foreign financing of the infrastructure investment. As I mentioned earlier, most of that goes to transportation and energy projects. Another issue is public guarantees. The share of commercial financing of infrastructure over time has declined, even when it is publicly guaranteed.

Figure 1 shows the stock of dispersed lending to infrastructure in billions of U.S. dollars over time. The upper block shows the total disbursement, and the lower block is publicly guaranteed private investment, which has declined. Even though people are talking more about private participation, real private flows are not coming in yet. In fact, they seem to have been declining in comparison to the total need. This raises an important problem of financing. If it is true that the private sector is not very interested in financing infrastructure, what can be done to increase it?

The last characteristic of this problem is demand, which is projected at $200 billion a year and is going to grow. It is already growing in three types of countries: countries that have just come out of macroeconomic adjustment, newly industrialized countries that are going through periods of rapid growth and have, at the moment, very congested infrastructure systems, and countries that are rapidly urbanizing. When you think about these three characteristics, you find they include almost the entire world, with very few exceptions. So the demand is certainly going to grow.

Why are we talking now about infrastructure financing? I want to go quickly through the advantages and disadvantages of the way infrastructure is financed at the moment, which is basically through public borrowing. Among the advantages, especially in developing countries, is that the government is sometimes the only credible entity in the country. For this kind of investment,

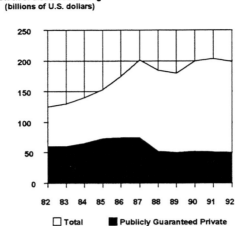

Stock of disbursed lending
(billions of U.S. dollars)

☐ Total   ■ Publicly Guaranteed Private

FIGURE 1 Publicly guaranteed private loans have fallen. Note: The loans are for electricity, gas, water, telecommunications, and transportation. Source: Adapted from World Development Report 1994 (The World Bank, 1994).

the government must play a role to establish credit worthiness. The second advantage is that governments can usually borrow at low rates, partly because of the certainty of repayment.

A disadvantage of government financing is that governments are usually more lax than the private sector in terms of financial discipline because they can always raise taxes or transfer funds to meet financial constraints.

Another disadvantage is that the government is not as efficient, partly because of the lack of financial discipline, but for other reasons as well, like overextension or the fact that civil servants of the infrastructure do not own the facilities for which they are responsible. Thus, there are inefficiencies, and these inefficiencies make government financing costly, even though borrowing may be at a lower rate than for the private sector. This puts a strain on government budgets, which is a real disadvantage.

A third disadvantage is that maintenance is usually neglected when the government is responsible for provision, at least in developing countries. I am not certain about the domestic experience, but I think it can be said that maintenance usually suffers. That is because the infrastructure is provided up front, paid for indirectly, generally by taxation, so users do not have a true sense of the cost. Maintenance is neglected because users do not have a sense of ownership of the infrastructure.

The overriding issue is that government financing is usually the best way to balance equity and efficiency issues. So the challenge becomes how to take advantage of the government but use the private sector to offset some of the elements that at the moment are disadvantages, the first one being financial discipline.

I am going to go over nine alternatives for financing infrastructure in order of increasing risk-sharing by the private sector. Bringing in the private sector is a question of keeping the advantages of government provision while allowing the private sector to take risks it normally would not take in order to make financing infrastructure feasible. Among the options are:

1. specially negotiated contributions
2. joint public/private companies
3. formal joint ventures
4. service delegation
5. leasing
6. concessioning
7. transferring responsibilities to the private sector
8. participation by users
9. privatization

The first alternative, specially negotiated contributions, are contributions negotiated once. The private sector brings in certain types of financing to put an infrastructure project together. Some countries have created mixed companies of joint public and private investment. There are formal joint ventures where the public and private sectors enter into formal contracts for one-time projects. Service delegation (the fourth alternative) is the transfer by government of planning and management responsibilities to private agents. The service is contracted out to the private sector, but the government keeps public ownership. There are various forms of transferring responsibilities to the private sector—participation, when users are given responsibility for financing and managing the infrastructure, and privatization, when there is a total transfer of ownership to the private sector.

These options differ in a number of ways, who owns the infrastructure at the end of the day, for example, which varies from the public sector to mixed ownership to completely private ownership. Another difference is who is responsible for planning. As you can see in figure 2, this varies depending on the option.

In the area of financing, the government could transfer responsibility but keep financing in the public sector for the efficiency of operations and to maintain the advantages of government borrowing and flexibility. The same arrangements can be made for operation and maintenance. I will describe these

TABLE 1 Responsibilities for Infrastructure Provision Under Alternative
Financing Arrangements

Option	Ownership	Planning	Financing	Operation and Maintenance
Specially Negotiated Contribution	public	public	private	public
Joint Public/Private Organizations	mixed	public	mixed	private
Formal Joint Ventures	mixed	public	private	private
Service Delegation	public	delegated agent	public	private
Contracting Out	public	public	public	private
Leasing	public	lessee	public	lessee
Concessioning	public	concessionaire	private	concessionaire
Participation by Users	users	users	users	users
Privatization	private	private	private	private

Source: Constructed from the 1994 World Development Report (The World
Bank, 1994); Urban Infrastructure: Finance and Management (OECD, 1991).

features, using examples from countries that have used one or another of these alternatives.

The first one is specially negotiated contributions which, I think, has also been used in the United States. The developer gives some contributions to infrastructure to finance things that would otherwise not have been financed. Usually that particular developer is interested in meeting some other, private goal.

In this case there are two examples, one from the United Kingdom and one from France. In the extension of the London Underground Railway in the United Kingdom, a developer provided the financing for developing the dock areas and make them more attractive. This was a very nice opportunity for expanding and improving the London underground. The key feature of the project was that it was a one-time, negotiated special contribution, not something to be repeated. The deal was arranged for that particular situation.

In France there is a more long-term arrangement, which has to do with urban density. Developers are given rights to provide higher density housing in certain areas of a city in return for some types of public infrastructure. The responsibility for managing the infrastructure remains in the hands of the cities. This arrangement has been in place since the 1970s. Interestingly, some cities have rejected this option as no longer feasible and have made it illegal, although it is still being used in other cities.

An example of joint public/private organizations, the second alternative method of financing, is the Trans-Tokyo Bay Highway in Japan. This is a very important 15-kilometer link into the existing network of highways in the metropolitan area. This project is a very interesting example of network infrastructure provided through private arrangements. The project was divided into two phases, the construction phase and the maintenance and operation phase. In the construction phase, the owner of the project remained the public sector, the Japan Highway Corporation, which also coordinated the project. The corporation also had responsibility for planning, administering and collecting tolls, financing the survey work, and purchasing the land. The private company was responsible for raising the capital for construction and managing the construction, at the end of which they handed over the completed project to the Japan Highway Corporation.

The most interesting aspect is in the maintenance and operation phase, when a new contract was negotiated and the Japan Highway Corporation paid the private entity through dedicated tolls collected by law. This is one way of financing the maintenance and operations. After this, the private and public companies have joint responsibility for maintaining and operating the highway.

The other example of a joint venture, called a "formal joint venture," although I have not come across an example of an informal joint venture because they are not reported, although they may exist. This case study is from

Australia, and the joint venture is between a state government and a private developer. The agreement is for urban infrastructure services.

The state government gives land and guarantees covering some elements of infrastructure, i.e., pipe connections and certain highway links. The private developer finances the construction and guarantees to provide infrastructure the state government does not provide, including low-income housing or housing for public allocation. What is interesting about this case is that the private and public sectors are sharing risks. That was a very good arrangement in terms of putting together this provision.

An example of service delegation, the fourth alternative, comes from Africa. In this case, agencies have been created in a number of countries. Recently this has also been done in Russia. A number of other non-African countries are adopting this approach, which involves governments transferring responsibility for planning and managing the procurement of public works to private agents. Agents have two responsibilities: to provide the infrastructure and to manage the implementation. So it is a dual agency.

The typical responsibilities of these agents include reviewing and selecting projects. Municipal governments and communities send project requests to the agent, and the agency reviews the projects and applies criteria agreed upon by the central government and the private agent on how to select projects. The selection of which projects are going to be financed is done by the private agent, which is very interesting. The second component of the service delegation arrangement is that the private agent finances the selected projects with funds from the central government. In other words, the agent manages the financing of this portfolio.

On the implementation side, the agent selects projects based on benefit-cost ratios and other criteria of social desirability. The agent manages the procurement or selects the winning bidder and manages the payments to the contractor, hires a firm to supervise the work, and manages other aspects of the government project. For example, governments in the following countries— Benin, Burkina Faso, Mali, Mauritania, Niger, Senegal, Chad, Gambia, and Madagascar—wanted to generate employment. So they put a private agent in charge of monitoring how many jobs are being created by various projects and documenting improvements in local construction industries. One of the objectives of these projects is that small-scale enterprises benefit from the investments.

The other example of service delegation is called contracting out. Although this practice is widespread in the United States, in developing countries it is usually limited to contracting out maintenance and operations. Here are a number of examples. In Pakistan, the railway company contracted out ticketing, cleaning, and catering for the railways, although everything else remained in the public sector. In Kenya, repair and maintenance of locomotives was contracted out. In the Philippines, in the port sector, the operation of an entire container terminal was contracted out.

In Chile, companies contract out reading meters and collecting fees for municipal water. This is interesting because in most developing countries municipal water companies are hampered by labor unions and are unable to restructure. Consequently, it is difficult for them to become more efficient. In some countries, municipal companies do not even know who their customers are because they do not have computerized systems, and people who have been working for the company for many years go from house to house to collect fees. If workers, civil servants, are the only ones who know who the customers are, it is very hard to improve efficiency. These are extreme problems, but metering and bill collection are difficult to improve through the public sector.

Another example of contracting out is in France, which has been so successful in contracting out public services that this model is called the "French model." Seventy percent of municipal water in France is contracted out, including management and operation of municipal systems and the treatment of waste. The municipalities maintain ownership of the assets, determine strategic policy in terms of investment, and regulate prices where there is no competition. (I think the exception is Paris, where there are two firms that have a yardstick competition.) The municipalities are also in charge of awarding contracts for management of these services and regulating the performance of the company.

The fifth alternative for financing infrastructure is leasing. An example is financing the water supply in Guinea, where the public sector plans and sets policy for the private sector, and is in charge of capital investments. The service company is a mixed public and private company, 49 percent of which is owned by the government. A foreign consortium owns the other 51 percent. The service company has a 10-year lease to provide services, mostly operation and maintenance. The company assumes the commercial risk—a very important feature of this arrangement—and is paid through user fees.

It is interesting to note that these arrangements can also involve foreign financing. For example, in the project for the water supply in Guinea, the negotiated agreement is between the government, a public/private company, and the external financier, the World Bank. The World Bank assumes declining shares of the foreign component of investment over time, and the central government assumes declining shares of debt. By the end of the lease period, which is 10 years, the public/private company would be responsible for the full capital investment. This was a key feature of the lease.

The sixth alternative is concessions, an example of which comes from Côte d'Ivoire. Here again, a French company, Saur, is involved. You can see why the French model is referred to in many situations where the public enterprise retains ownership of the infrastructure, but responsibilities are transferred to the private company (the seventh alternative). In this case, the ownership of capital is as follows: the local interest is 52 percent; the foreign interest is 46 percent, through the French private firm; and the government interest is 2 percent.

The Côte d'Ivoire project is a concession contract, (the seventh alternative) under which the investment and operational responsibility for supplying water for the whole country, not just the city, is given to the private company. The contract has a provision for investments in low-income areas, and specifies what the company should do in terms of providing services to low-income housing—waiving the connection charge. The company assumes the social responsibility for this provision.

Tariffs, which are set by the company, must meet a number of objectives—operating costs, money for expanding and rehabilitating the networks, paying the shareholders, and paying the government a rental fee (because the government had accumulated a lot of debt in the past and wanted to repay it). On top of paying taxes, the company was responsible for debt payment.

Despite the tall order of what the tariffs have to cover, the company has been realizing a 5 to 6 percent growth rate in connections, including low-income housing connections. The performance has improved, and unaccounted-for-water is less than 15 percent, which, I believe, is less than in the metropolitan Washington area. Collection from private consumers has never gone below 98 percent, which is dramatic. Only public service users are not paying at the moment, which is a very interesting difference. The company is now down to four staff people per thousand connections, which is a very good level of performance. The tariffs are the same as in neighboring countries. Because they improved efficiency, tariffs have not gone up. This is an example of a successful leasing out arrangement.

Another leasing arrangement is a little bit different because it involves participation by users, the eighth alternative. This is an example of an important way of including private investments. This case is from Peru, where there are a number of water user associations to whom the government has given—without charge—the responsibility for managing all of the irrigation infrastructure. The government provides technical assistance on how to carry out the operation and maintenance, and poor communities receive grants for expanding irrigation systems. The government also manages the auctioning of rights, which are tradable. The government manages the auction so user associations can sell their rights.

User associations can borrow money, but at commercial rates, and they can only borrow for new investments or rehabilitation. They are not allowed to borrow for maintenance. The associations design the projects and execute them, repay the loans (sometimes in kind by providing labor). They also provide labor and operate and maintain the infrastructure.

For the last option, privatization, I am not going to use specific examples. You can see in table 1 the scale of privatization that has already taken place. About 25 countries have now undertaken huge transfers of ownership of infrastructure. For more detail, you can consult "Infrastructure for Development," in the World Development Report published by the World Bank in 1994.

I want to list a number of concerns about privatization. These have to do with who should own the assets in the case of private financing, how to do investment planning and coordinate activities, who sets policies, whether or not there is regulation, who manages capital financing, who manages current financing, how to deal with operations and maintenance, who has managerial authority over the system, who bears what risk and how to make sure risks are properly borne, and how to compensate private parties that undertake the investments. Also how long should the contract be?

On the resource side there are, as I mentioned earlier, various infrastructure development funds; infrastructure funds, if they exist; and domestic capital markets. The macroeconomic implications of these vary according to country. How good is the existing managerial and technical

TABLE 2 Value of Infrastructure Privatizations in Developing Countries (in millions of U.S. dollars)

	1988	1989	1990	1991	1992	Total 1988-92	Number of Countries
Telecommunications	325	212	4036	5743	1504	11820	14
Power generation	106	2100	20	248	1689	4163	9
Power distribution	0	0	0	98	1037	1135	2
Gas distribution	0	0	0	0	1906	1906	2
Railroads	0	0	0	110	217	327	1
Road infrastructure	0	0	250	0	0	250	1
Ports	0	0	0	0	7	7	2
Water	0	0	0	0	175	175	2
Airlines	367	42	775	168	1461	2813	14
Shipping	0	0	0	135	1	136	2
Road transport	0	0	0	1	12	13	3
Total	798	2354	5081	6503	8009	22745	15
Total developing country privatizations	2587	5188	8618	2204	23187	61629	25

Source: Compiled from the World Development Report 1994 (The World Bank, 1994)

capacity? Can the private sector be involved efficiently? Does the private sector have an interest and, if not, how can they be made more interested?

Not all public sectors guarantee competition among private providers, in which case we face the monopoly issues Dr. Brennan talked about. There are also questions about characteristics of the service and how the service is being used. For the private good? For the public good? There are a number of concerns there. Then there is the issue of equity, which is difficult to deal with, and also environmental concerns. All of these factors affect the potential success and selection of various financing options.

Note: The World Bank does not accept responsibility for the views expressed herein, which are those of the author and should not be attributed to The World Bank or to its affiliated organizations. The findings, interpretations, and conclusions are results of research supported by the Bank; they do not necessarily represent official policy of the Bank. The designation employed, the presentation of material, and any maps used in the document are purely for the convenience of the reader and do not imply the expression of any opinion whatsoever on the part of the World Bank or its affiliates concerning the legal status of any country, territory, city, area, or of its authorities, or concerning the delimitations of its boundaries or national affiliation.

Current Issues in Infrastructure Finance

Natalie R. Cohen
Fiscal Stress Monitor

I owe my presence here today to the gnatcatcher, a small bird that likes to dance around wildly as it catches insects. Its endangerment had slowed down construction of the $1.1 billion San Joaquin Hills Toll Road in Orange County, California. Anticipation of protests of this construction project by environmental groups led managers to put a large contingency into the financing consisting of about $100 million and two years of extra capitalized interest beyond the expected completion date of March 1997 to account for environmentally caused delay. Little did they know that those contingency funds would come in handy to cover an $81 million loss on their invested construction funds as well as loss of projected interest earnings as a result of the Orange County debacle.

I wrote about this in an issue of *Infrastructure Finance*, which ultimately led me here. I am going to speak a little bit more about the Orange County consequences for infrastructure finance later, but I would like first to share a few general views about infrastructure finance today.

In my opinion, infrastructure finance is lagging today. At the state and local level, I do not believe that in the near future there is going to be a tremendous amount of attention given to financing the infrastructure in the current political and economic environment. I am going to outline a few of the reasons. Certainly, with efforts in Congress to balance the budget, new infrastructure initiatives are not likely to come from the federal government either right now. However, infrastructure financing is receiving some attention in pockets of the country where economic growth is quite healthy. I think it is important not just to paint a broad brush picture of infrastructure problems, but to look also at some pockets that are experiencing a natural evolution of infrastructure growth through the private sector creation of capital, jobs, and wealth. I am going to end with some of those bright spots.

I would like to present some of the reasons I do not think there is going to be a rush to finance infrastructure projects at the local level in the next few years. First, as more social services are downloaded or devolved from the federal government to the state and local level, the grab for local dollars is going to intensify. The last devolution took place early in the Reagan years, and it is instructive to look at that time to help explain state and local behavior today. Second, with more competition for local dollars, pressure on local tax rates obviously has also intensified. In reaction, taxpayers are protesting. Our federal system is set up so taxpayers have much more opportunity to vote their wishes directly for government at the state and local level than at the federal level. As a result, tax limitations, caps, incentives, and referenda are alive and well today. Finally, the key revenue source at the local level, the property tax, is under fire. Some of the reasons for this, and I will get into this, are immutable demographic and economic trends that are likely to continue.

Let's take the first point. In the early 1980s, Congress passed President Reagan's program for economic recovery, which transformed many federal categorical programs into block grants, cut funding levels, and handed them over to state and local governments, much like what is happening today. At that time, the devolution coincided with the end of the 1982–1983 recession. The nation's economy had taken off sharply just about the time when the effect of the federal cuts was being felt. With surplus funds accumulating in many state coffers, state and local governments were only too happy to take over some of the social programs the federal government was unloading.

For seven straight years state governments increased their budgets 8 percent for each year or, after inflation, 3.2 percent annually. Swollen budgets and expanded social programs left the states poorly positioned to handle the recession that hit us in the early 1990s. The early 1990s on the state and local government level was marked by mid-year crises, spending reductions, cuts at the state level of aid to local governments, and tax increases. A number of states saw their credit ratings chopped. Record tax rate increases led to voter unrest, and ultimately, a number of stringent tax limitations were voted in.

One of the first items to go during a fiscal crisis is the capital budget, in some measure through deferred maintenance, postponed borrowing, and pushing capital products out into the later years of a capital plan. The relationship between fiscal stress and reduced capital spending has been well documented. I also know it directly from experience, having worked for New York City's Office of Management and Budget in the late 1970s.

Looking at this a little bit differently, from the perspective of the national income and product accounts, you can see that there was a shift during the expansionary 1980s away from capital spending towards social service spending at the state and local government levels. The national income and product accounts accounting includes expenditures and revenues of the current fiscal year, excludes bond proceeds but includes interest on state and local debt, and also includes capital outlays. It is an interesting snapshot.

Measured this way, accounts show that the deficits of state and local governments grew from $3 billion at the end of 1986 to about $30 billion in the first half of 1990. Deficits of this magnitude had not been seen since the 1974 recession. They were common during the 1950s and 1960s when capital spending for roads, schools, and other infrastructure made up about 25 percent of outlays. However, the deficits of the 1980s did not reflect a surge in capital spending. Rather, outlays for construction remained consistently at about 10 percent through the latter part of the 1980s, down from about 25 percent during the last surge in capital spending.

These findings are consistent with the assumption that state and local governments did pick up and expand social service programs during this time period. Ironically, the deficits appeared during a time of general economic expansion and continued to get worse although there was no general economic downturn, which I believe is why the recession in the early 1990s hurt local governments so drastically.

Today similar measures by the federal government for block grants for welfare and to hand other social programs over to the states have made it through Congress. Some states again have seen their first surpluses since the recession in the early 1990s. Whether or not those states choose to pick up where the federal government leaves off remains to be seen. Today's statehouses are vastly different from what they were in the 1980s. There is more concern today with keeping taxes low and managing and controlling spending than with expanding services.

At best, however, state legislatures will be tremendously preoccupied with how to manage their new responsibilities. Whether it is Medicaid, welfare, or criminal justice, considerable discussion will focus on getting programs set up, managed, and monitored. At worst, the impulse to download further, from the state level to the local level, will also become stronger, which, no matter how you slice it, leaves a lot less air time for infrastructure projects.

This brings me to my second point about why infrastructure will have a tough time in today's political environment. One outlet, as I have touched on before, for some of the local fiscal pressure has been citizen taxpayer protest. The record for the most citizen-initiated petitions since 1934 was broken in 1990. Taxpayer unrest is alive and well at the local level. Local government is one of the few arenas, as I mentioned earlier, where taxpayers can directly vent their frustrations with government. Many states have authorized direct citizen-initiated referenda, and it is typical for taxpayers to vote local bond issues and budgets. Unfortunately, we do not get to vote the annual federal budget or vote directly for the level of federal taxes or federal borrowing.

Another reason taxpayer frustrations are expressed at the local level has to do with some of the changes in property ownership, which brings me to my third point. Property taxes are a key source of revenue for local governments. The demographic profile of property owners is changing, and this trend, I believe, is likely to continue. In the last decade, we have witnessed one of the worst declines of all time in property wealth. Property wealth expanded greatly during the 1970s, but during the 1980s growth and values ground to a halt, ending the decade at virtually the same level where it began.

Commercial property fared a little bit better in the 1980s than owner-occupied housing with values just shy of 2 percent higher at the end of the 1980s than at the beginning. In contrast, the value of owner-occupied housing—and again this is a macro figure—fell 6 percent. These numbers are all after inflation.

In the first three years of the 1990s, owner-occupied housing fell about 2.2 percent in value while commercial property lost 26 percent in value. Add to this a very important shift in the makeup of residential homeowners. Today's residential property homeowner is more likely to be over 65 and less likely to have children at home than 10 years ago. No wonder the property tax is under fire, particularly for schools and spending for education. The only age group with a greater share of home ownership than 10 years ago is the over 65 set.

The percentage of homeowners between 25 and 64 declined from 77 percent in 1981 to 74 percent in 1991. The proportion of homeowners who were over 65 grew, in contrast, from about 22 percent to 26 percent. If you are over 65, you are more likely to live in your own home than you were 10 years ago. If you are between 25 and 64, you are less likely to own your own home than you were 10 years ago.

The proportion of owner-occupied households with children under 18 was about 40 percent in 1981. By 1991 this number had fallen to about 36 percent. The proportion of school-aged children living in rental housing has grown from about 25 percent in 1981 to about 30 percent today. I believe this explains why some bond issues for education and school district spending are being voted down.

Although the baby boomlet is with us, children today are less represented by property-tax-paying homeowners than they were a decade ago. Aging homeowners today are (a) facing losses in property values, (b) living on fixed retirement incomes, and (c) paying higher property taxes to meet growing social needs. Putting these together, it is easy to understand why there is a movement to shrink local government.

Another key characteristic of the over-65-year-old homeowner is that he or she is significantly mobile. Unlike some other social spending programs, Social Security is portable, and it is a commonly accepted cultural practice to make a geographical move for retirement. The mobility of retirees is a very important national trend. Retirees feel that they have postponed certain joys until this time in their lives, and they very strongly want things their way.

Migrating retirees are contributing to some of the growth today in rural counties as they move there looking for greater safety, a lower cost of living, and a slower pace than in the denser population centers where they earned their money for retirement. The new immigrant to some of these communities is less likely to be loyal or feel a connection to the local government and its particular needs. In this context, prospects for revenue and user-fee-supported projects look a little bit brighter than for traditional property-tax-supported projects.

The Orange County toll road financing is an interesting example of this trend. With the dearth of new California debt but significantly eager investor demand, the Foothill Eastern Transportation Corridor Agency was able to market successfully a $1.3 billion toll road revenue bond at the end of May 1995. The issue sold very well, and it was rated investment grade by Standard and Poors and Fitch Investor Service. An investment grade rating is unusual for a toll road with no operating history, especially in the context of the Orange County, California, bankruptcy. Apparently Orange County residents are unwilling to pay a half a cent increase in their sales tax for general government, but they are willing to pay tolls to make commuting faster and smoother.

Other capital projects in Orange County are not likely to do as well. Like New York City's fiscal crisis in the 1970s, the disinvestment by local government in the infrastructure will only begin to unfold in Orange County in the next two years. Since the bankruptcy filing, real estate values are down by about 20 percent. New housing construction has nearly ground to a halt, and resales are difficult. Certain capital projects were canceled completely. It is difficult to imagine that there is room at all in the budget for any capital improvement projects at the county level. The recovery plan that they put together also diverts money from the transportation authority and from other local governments in the county, which, needless to say, means governments must tighten their spending belts considerably.

I promised that I would mention a number of bright spots to conclude. In some locations in this country where private sector development is intense, new infrastructure is being built. The recent boom in technology has a number of cities, towns, and counties growing at a rapid pace. Take North Sioux City, South Dakota, for example, the home of the Gateway 2000 Computer Company. The city had a population of 200 not long ago. They are now struggling to meet the needs of 4,000 Gateway 2000 Computer employees. I spoke with the corporate communications director there, and she said that on many days she has to walk a mile to a mile and a half from her car in the parking lot to her office. Housing there is in short supply. They are rapidly building roads. They just put in a brand new sewer system. The Sioux City, Iowa, airport, which serves the region, has been expanded and can now accommodate jets, whereas they could not before.

Another example is Rio Rancho, New Mexico, which has been written up a little bit in recent history. Rio Rancho was once a bedroom community of Albuquerque. It is now attracting reverse commuters for some of the job growth there. Rio Rancho is home to one of Intel's new semiconductor chip plants, and it is also home to the technical support center for the software maker Intuit. Taco Bell houses their accounting division there.

Advances in telecommunications have enabled real-time links between remote rural locations and the rest of the world. Midwestern and plains states once suffering under the weight of the farm crisis are now experiencing a vast turnaround. They are seeing some of the lowest unemployment nationally. In some locations, unemployment is below 2 percent, and even in the 1 percent range in some communities.

Housing, roads, sewers, water systems, and airports are all experiencing dramatic growth in these regions. These changes have challenged our traditional assumptions about the viability of the growth potential of rural and small communities. If technological advances and smart economic development are inspiring solutions to some of the classic problems in remote rural locations, we ought to be able to come up with ideas to solve the infrastructure problems of older urban centers.

Discussion of the Morning Presentations

Participant: How does the widening income disparity in this country change the calculation of future benefits of infrastructure—when you have one group who are, indeed, enjoying the benefits of a very fast pace of American entrepreneurialism and investment and another group who seem to be sliding further and further away from that. Certainly one reflection of that is, perhaps, the decline in home ownership or the wealth of home ownership as a whole.

Dr. Brennan: There are just a couple of brief comments I would like to make on that. One is that income disparity does not change the general thrust of the question about whether opportunity cost or equal standing is the right way to evaluate long-term infrastructure investments. What disparity adds to this already complicated question is that one may have to worry about the incidence of the costs and the incidence of the benefits, in other words, who loses and who gains. Are we obligated to have wealthy people fund investments now that will benefit poorer people later, poorer people elsewhere (in deciding who gets World Bank funding), or poorer people here and now?

There is a standard economist response to disparity issues, which is not to worry about it now because, if we maximize the size of the pie, we can take care of the size of the slices at some point later on. That response may not be too realistic. Given the feasible alternatives we have in front of us, we probably ought to take income disparity into account.

The second comment, which I think other people here are more qualified to speak about than I am, concerns the effects of wealth distribution on the flexibility issues Ms. Everett brought up. There is one school of thought that says that if wealth gets concentrated in the hands of a small number of people, they are easier to soak by a poorer majority in a democracy. There is another school of thought that says that smallness is actually a political virtue because it makes it easier to organize more effectively. If I had to guess which is true, I would say that the second is more likely to hold than the first. Perhaps that is a cynical view of the state of affairs these days, but other people can discuss that. The questions are probably even more pronounced in the developing countries that Dr. Humplick talked about.

Ms. Cohen: I can throw some demographic figures out. I do think this is an important issue. I think the disparity in wealth is generational, and that is what I find to be a disturbing trend between the older generation and the younger generation coming up today. I have a few statistics on that because I have done research on some of the demographic changes in the 1980s. Despite the fact that the baby boom generation is now roughly in its peak earning years, median household income is only about 3 percent higher than it was a decade ago, and this is after adjusting for inflation.

There was a 50 percent jump in the number of households within the 35- to 44-year-old range, family years, etc., but income of the baby bust generation fell 10 percent over their age counterparts of 10 years earlier. There has been, as many of us are aware, particularly in the urban centers, a dramatic increase in the number of young female heads of households with small children living at or below the poverty level. Obviously, the willingness and ability of these households as they mature in age to support state and local government programs is going to be challenged in the near future.

Dr. Brennan: I would just like to add something quickly to that about the group that was not mentioned, senior citizens. There is a myth that they are the poorest people in the country. But they are the wealthiest. They tend to own their own homes. Social Security and Medicare have been enormous successes for redistributing income toward the elderly in this country.

Dr. Bugliarello: We are talking about private wealth, if you like, but there is also public wealth that accumulates from generation to generation. Highways and airports are public wealth. So, the new generation has more public libraries, etc., than the previous one. How is that taken into account? In other words, my wealth is my personal wealth, whatever that may be, but also a share of the public wealth. I may be privately not very well off, but I enjoy the advantages of an environment that has been built over several generations. Is this a significant factor to be considered, and, if so, how?

Dr. Humplick: I may try to address the two separate questions. On the question of public wealth, what seems to be the case, according to our coefficients, is that you may inherit this very rich stock of public wealth, but it has huge maintenance costs. And so you may actually be poorer as a result because to maintain it is a responsibility. So that is one of the concerns.

In terms of income disparity, having the private sector pick up some of the financing for public works gives the public sector more resources to deal with income disparity. In a sense, you transfer the responsibility for provisions to the private sector to get the efficiency gain, and that leaves the budget free for addressing social issues. So there is an opportunity to rebalance the role of the public sector in taking up social responsibilities and leaving the provision responsibilities for goods to the private sector. That may allow us to address these income disparities in the future and at present.

Ms. Everett: Yes, but there is still a move away from the activist tone that you might have seen represented in congressional reports of say 10 years ago. In the U.S. House of Representatives report there is a real sense that the federal government's role will have to be changed, that it is going to be smaller than it has been in the past, and that state and local governments and the private sector are going to have to do more. I will say, however, that there is a more optimistic tone in the congressional report than there is in the U.S. Army Corps of Engineers report.

Participant: It is rather interesting that much of the rhetoric about not investing in future infrastructure implies an unwillingness to obligate our grandchildren, when in actuality it appears much more that not wanting to spend at all is the principal reason. We have inherited a great deal of infrastructure investment, but we seem, perhaps for the first time, to have no inclination to carry on that investment. We want to stop now and consume it. I fear the concern is not so much about obligating our grandchildren as it is with not wanting to spend our own money today because that would diminish what we have available in the present. After we are gone, we are like your tulip people. We do not care what happens. That is very troubling to me because it seems what we really have is a lack of willingness to invest in the future under the guise of not wanting to obligate the future.

Ms. Connery: You know there is, if I may just interject, a dimension to this that has not been mentioned here that I think bears investigation. Infrastructure is sort of talked about as one great amorphous thing. But there is at least one major differentiation, besides the modes of transportation and all the services, and that is the infrastructure that could be called productive infrastructure. That is the infrastructure that takes goods to market, gets people to work, does very specific things on behalf of job creation, wealth creation, and so on.

There is a whole other dimension of infrastructure loosely called "social overhead capital." This includes both environmental improvements and amenities, the things that we tend to lump together in America as part of one great category called infrastructure. In fact, infrastructure is differentiated very clearly in other countries, not only in the developing countries but I think even in countries like Japan.

I was struck by Ms. Everett's reference to the report that compared us to Japan, which I think is totally fallacious because, in fact, they historically put their investment into productive infrastructure at the cost of not investing in social overhead capital. They are now trying to catch up in a very hard way because land there is very costly. It is also very difficult to do that after development has taken place.

It would be interesting to me to find out whether or not in the United States we are beginning to differentiate and see whether the same level of investment is going in to keep business happy because there is a lot of strong lobbying on behalf of business. But the social overhead capital, the amenities, the libraries for instance, the environmental controls, which are beginning to be threatened fairly seriously by cutbacks, may in fact be diminished. That sets up a number of other equity issues and interesting dimensions that I have not really thought very much about, but I suddenly became very interested in today.

Participant: On the subject of educating the public, I think the public does not know about the condition of the infrastructure, as well as not caring. I think when they see a TV special on it, they are concerned about how many bridges have problems. I think there is a lot to infrastructure that the public really does not know about, and if they do not know they cannot make a determination whether or not they care.

Dr. Humplick: I think the historical way in which infrastructure has been financed partially contributes to this in the sense that it has been financed through general taxation, for the most part, and people do not keep account of what happens to their taxes the same way they keep account of what happens to their out-of-pocket costs. Because of that, the awareness of what you are spending and how it is being used is lower in the case of general taxation than it is in the case of direct charges.

This is, I think, one of the contributing reasons people seem to be unaware of infrastructure spending and, therefore, do not care about where it is going and what is going to happen in the future. The other thing has something to do with the category of infrastructure that we normally talk about. It has this huge initial investment, to a large extent, and then it lives for a long time. In that period it rarely needs much.

What the infrastructure needs is hardly thought about until it suddenly is not there. This makes the catastrophic view of thinking about infrastructure the current view in the sense that people are only aware of infrastructure when it fails. This is a characteristic that can rarely be changed because it is inherent in infrastructure. But when people become more aware of the infrastructure in the way that they are aware of their private assets, they start to think about it in that way.

Having infrastructure is like having your own house that needs a new roof every so many years. If people felt the same sense of relationship to the infrastructure, they would also be more responsive toward paying for its care and more aware of how it is being maintained. I think the challenge to policymakers and also to people who are responsible for infrastructure in general is to somehow link the financing of infrastructure to ownership of it. Ownership does not have to be in the real sense of contributing toward financing but in thinking about it as something that you actually have a stake in. The environmental lobby has been very good at making people aware of forests and owls. I think infrastructure needs a similar approach.

Participant: I was struck by what Ms. Cohen said about the rise of the Gateway 2000 Company in Sioux City and the implications of that for infrastructure. It seems that the communications we have now and the speed of commercial change allow companies like Gateway to grow extremely rapidly. But also when a company grows rapidly like that, it can quickly go bust. We have seen many large computer companies flourish for a few years then die away very quickly. In the past, when we developed infrastructure in a rural area, it might be for mining or for farming, which had an extended potential lifetime.

I am not sure what the arrangements for building the infrastructure in Sioux City are, but you have to bring a public/private arrangement that is going to build infrastructure to meet the need right now but with an uncertain future. Five years from now there may be a few bad reports on Gateway computers, and their sales may go way down; they could even go bankrupt. Then you have an infrastructure built in an area in a place where it may be very difficult to find somebody to come in and utilize it right away.

Dr. Bugliarello: Just to respond very quickly, I believe there is another point. The infrastructure being built there is at the expense of infrastructure that could have been built in another place or was already in place. We have been doing this throughout the country. Essentially, we neglect the infrastructure in certain regions, while building infrastructure from scratch in new regions. We are expanding infrastructure more than, perhaps, we should were it not for the fact that from the economic, production, and industrial viewpoint it is apparently better in certain cases to build a new infrastructure, in Sioux City, say, than to add to the infrastructure of Pittsburgh.

Participant: I was wondering if any of you had a comment about whether or not there is a credibility problem with the money coming down to Washington for obligated trust funds and Congress not spending the surplus on the very projects they were intended to fund?

Dr. Humplick: One of the reasons I did not talk about funds of that sort is because, within the World Bank and also within the family of economists, there is no agreement as to whether earmarking is good or bad from a macroeconomic point of view. That is one of the main reasons I think trust funds as such have not been very useful for financing infrastructure. Although they give the user the direct view of where fees are going in terms of financing, trust funds reduce the flexibility of the government to deal with short-term problems and reallocate public funds in the short term.

I think that separation between the government's flexibility to manage allocations and the direct link to users and what is happening to their fees is the problem. Many countries that have put together highway trust funds or road funds are facing these problems at the moment because users like them very much. Users are very happy to see where their fees are going, but the central government loses flexibility in allocating funds across sectors.

Dr. Brennan: I suspect the American public does not have much of a problem with credibility regarding trust fund distributions, just because I doubt that a very high percentage of the public knows anything about trust funds. If there is a credibility problem, it may affect people who are in the road-building or construction industries. They expected there would be demand for these businesses, generated by the trust funds, which is not there because the government is not doing with the trust funds what they expected it to do with them. I doubt that there is a lot of clamoring by the general public to recall representatives because of the trust funds, however.

Ms. Everett: I second that. I tend to think the American public does not know what is being done with trust funds. I think a bigger or an additional problem is that it is not just the Congress that is distorting the subject, but also the Office of Management and the Budget. It is useful for the Office of Management and the Budget right now to consider these monies as part of the unified budget.

Participant: With all this depressing information—the budget figures coming out of the Republican Congress, left wing and right wing politics on the environment and income distribution—is there any way we can fund transportation infrastructure now, or should we just let it fall apart and prepare for 6 or 10 years down the road?

Ms. Connery: I think you have made an interesting point because, in fact, whether you are right or left, Democrat or Republican, liberal or conservative, you drive every day. More and more, there is an astonishing level of increase in the vehicle miles traveled, the basic measure of how much we get out there. Obviously, there are lots of concerns about that, and I share them, but I think we have to look at the fact that ultimately our livelihoods and our lives depend on our mobility, particularly as we form smaller and smaller households with more complex needs. Women are out there more and more with careers as well as family, which factors into that.

Your question is can we find a way of at least establishing a common ground to go forward on this. I fear for my own state right now, which is the state of Maine. Where I live, we are funding less than half of our maintenance budget for transportation. We can see the effects of that right now in bridge deterioration to the point where my husband, who is a politician, appears at meetings with the department of transportation wearing a life preserver to let them know that this is important.

Beyond the theatrics, it is a serious problem. At some point I think we can find common ground. It has to do with staging the debate differently. Some of the efforts I would cite are the New Jersey Alliance for Action, which is attempting to cast the debate in terms understandable across the political spectrum. There are others, the Regional Planning Association of New York, which represents New York, New Jersey, and Connecticut, and the I-95 Coalition. None of them alone is going to change the nature of the debate, but I take heart from the fact that they are thinking beyond just immediate self-interest. They are framing the debate in ways that reach the middle ground and ultimately look at not only immediate needs but also longer term needs.

Participant: I think there is a place for trust funds. If you put out a six-year authorization of the trust fund, and you make some commitment that the money will be there and place it out of the reach of politics, there are a lot of people who are willing to make investments and make million-dollar decisions based on those trust funds, which is good for growth. I think it is okay to look at trust funds from a pro-business standpoint.

Dr. Humplick: I agree with you. When I made my comment, it is because the experience with trust funds has been very mixed. Most countries facing budget deficits have found trust funds to be very inflexible, and they have tried ways of moving away from having them managed by the public sector and having them belong to users. Road-user associations have been formed to take over the management of road funds, for example. That has worked very well in making the financing of the fund function more directly as a user fee because users are part of the membership that manages the fund in a more direct way than through a trust fund that is managed federally or centrally.

I think there are ways to reduce the effects of earmarking and removing flexibility from federal hands, which is what a fund does, and keeping the efficiency of using those funds directly for financing the infrastructure they were supposed to finance in the first place. It is a very delicate balance, and countries with deficits have a lot of trouble dealing with that. One can argue that road infrastructure may not be the priority for that particular year. There may be other priorities, like health and education and so on. So the short-term optimization is forsaken when you have earmarked funds.

As I said, there is no agreement as to which is worse. Is it worse to let infrastructure deteriorate and then pay 20 times more to replace it than to maintain it periodically using a fund? Or is it worse to lose flexibility of period-by-period optimization across sectors? For the economy, it is hard to quantify the differences between these two options. This is why I personally cannot say, based on the experience we have, which one is better. For roads or for any infrastructure that has a fund, it is better for that infrastructure to have the fund. But for the economy as a whole it is hard to say. That is the difficult point.

Ms. Everett: Apparently this Congress and the American public cannot hold in their minds at the same time the two ideas of reducing the deficit and promoting greater economic wealth. I have to think that at a certain point there will be pressures that will lead us to undertake the greater investment. Those pressures will have to do with how we are going to take care of our sluggish, long-term economic growth problem, get to a higher production curve, and take care of the disparity of income in our country. I think these are looming problems. Also, at some point, reinvestment in our nation's cities has got to become a preoccupation. Sooner or later I think this thing will turn around, and we will look at infrastructure investment as a valuable component of dealing with all of these problems. I just see this as a temporary preoccupation with contraction.

Dr. Brennan: Carol's response gets to a question I was asked earlier about capital budgeting accounts. I think, as is true with accounting in general, capital budgeting does not necessarily tell us in a direct way how to act. But it may affect what we think, i.e., what we can or cannot hold in our heads when we make decisions. It may be okay to run deficits to pay for things when the benefits last a long time, thus spreading the payments out over time. To the extent that capital budgeting helps us think more clearly about these things and has feedback effects of the type we are describing, it can be useful.

Ms. Cohen: One comment on the transportation question. I presented a lot of depressing statistics, but maybe I am basically an optimist. I thought the $1.3 billion Foothill Eastern bond sale was a phenomenal statement of the importance of transportation to people. It is phenomenal to receive an investment grade rating for a yet-to-be-built toll road. I have worked for a rating agency and a bond insurance company, and you just never ever would consider that toll road investment grade because of the construction risk, especially in the context of an environmental and political culture where there are going to be fights and delays.

People want transportation, and they are willing to pay for it. The confidence was there. The people are going to pay for it even though Orange County is bankrupt. They had just voted down a sales tax increase for general government to bail out some of their problems. Real estate is falling through the floor, etc., etc.

Commuting times are essentially the same today in the Washington, D.C., metropolitan area as they were 20 years ago despite the incredible differences in distances people travel. People are out there building, jobs are being created, and so on. Anyhow, I leave you with that statistic.

Technology, Infrastructure, and Competitiveness in a National Innovation System

Deborah L. Wince-Smith
Council on Competitiveness

Although this colloquium deals with the financing of and the challenges to physical infrastructures, i.e., constructed buildings and transportation, etc., I want to give you a little broader perspective on national innovation and where this particular issue of the infrastructure falls. Also, I want to talk about how other matters that affect the ability of the United States to create national wealth and train highly skilled workers affect the infrastructure. I am going to speak rather broadly and hope that I will engender some discussion before the afternoon session.

I think we all recognize that innovation in the private sector is a requisite to national productivity and economic growth. Individual investment decisions of private enterprises ultimately affect our national economic strength. The government, as we know, has a strong interest in ensuring that business capital flows into areas that promote long-term growth, productivity, and the creation of wealth. But at the end of the day, the private sector has to translate whatever national assets we have into wealth-generating activities.

Currently, there is much discussion in the science and technology community, on the issue of government and private sector roles and responsibilities in the support of research and development (R&D) and overall competitiveness. There has been some discussion of direct fiscal incentives, such as the research and experimentation (R&E) tax credit, and much discussion of the federal investment in civilian, commercially oriented technology, or cost-shared R&D partnering. But there has not been a lot of discussion of the network of impediments, disincentives, and special interests, which, I believe, collectively stifle the ability of American firms to reap the benefits of our national leadership in science and technology and our dynamic, entrepreneurial culture.

I want to give you a framework for a national innovation system and then look at both the disincentives and potential incentives for us to capitalize on as we move into the next century. The United States, in spite of what you may hear from those who are worried about the level of government investments in R&D, spends more on R&D than France, Germany, the United Kingdom, and Japan combined. We spend a tremendous amount in the government environment on R&D, and we also spend a tremendous amount in the private sector, cumulatively between $160 billion and $170 billion. Because a robust R&D technology base is important to the economic issues I have mentioned, the federal government, at least since World War II, has been providing direct support for what we classically refer to as basic research.

Economists Michael Boskin and Lawrence Lau have estimated in a recent paper, "The Contribution of R&D to Economic Growth," that the introduction of new technology has accounted for 30 to 50 percent of economic growth. So government investment in the seed corn—the basic research and underlying infrastructure, if you will, of knowledge creation—has been very important.

In the last 15 years, we have seen a change in government policies, inching toward much closer interaction between private sector users of technology and government supporters of technology for mission purposes through, among other things, public/private cost-shared partnerships.

The Clinton administration made the concept of public/private partnerships a cornerstone of its technology policy, building on many of the initiatives from the last two years of the Reagan/Bush era. In a simplistic sense, the philosophy came down to this. If we would just restructure the priorities of the federal R&D system, cut back expenditures for national security and defense and mission work in general, have more civilian-oriented technology development, and do this through cost-shared partnerships or direct grant programs such as the Advanced Technology Program to create more commercially oriented technology, we would become world class competitors. I want to argue that this philosophy does not ensure global competitiveness for the United States. So, let me go through the elements of a technology innovation system and how to create a system that is relevant for the next century.

Successful technology innovation depends upon one very simple thing. It depends upon a private sector entity—either in a small, medium, or large firm or a collaboration—taking a knowledge or technology asset developed indigenously, in partnership with the government or with other firms, and quickly and cost efficiently translating it into a competitive new or improved product or service. What do private sector entities do with the knowledge or technology asset? They obtain market share.

Market share is really the final determinant of whether or not you have been successful. And in today's global economy, the market share is not just domestic but global—capturing the product and service end-user markets on a world wide basis. Clearly, in the construction industry, every major U.S. firm operates globally. The growth markets are not just in the United States. They are all over the world. Think of the tremendous physical infrastructure challenges in the former Soviet Union. There are similar challenges and opportunities in China.

I will mention one that I have become a little familiar with, the Three Gorges Project. I do not know if any of you are familiar with this major initiative now under way in China. U.S. construction firms are very interested in the initiative and eager to participate in it. At the moment, however, I think we are the only advanced industrial democracy that is not moving forward with any government support for such participation. Even the Canadians, who like to think of themselves as far more environmentally oriented than we are, have strongly endorsed the Three Gorges Project and are providing direct financing subsidies to their major construction firms. Right now the Export-Import Bank is not able to do that for American firms because of guidelines from the White House. I mention this as an example of a global market and the importance of the market share beyond our own backyard.

NATIONAL TECHNOLOGY INNOVATION SYSTEM

What are the elements of the national technology innovation system? The first element is the human resource base. A nation needs skilled, educated people. That is obvious, but it is of great concern to the United States. Even though we spend more money on education per pupil, per capita, than any other country in the world, many of us feel that the quality and the delivery of our national public education system are sorely wanting.

I will share a few very sad statistics. There are more school administrators in New York City than in all of France. There are more school administrators in New York State than in the entire European community. Anyone who has small children knows that, even if you live in purportedly affluent parts of the country, first grade classes are now held in trailers. There are just not enough resources to do the things we all took for granted growing up in a time when all these national financial resources did not go into education. That is not clearly an infrastructure issue in the sense that you have been talking about, but I put the human resource base as the primary element for an innovation system.

Second, there is the technology asset. Fundamental new knowledge, technology know-how, and other R&D assets are necessary but insufficient for commercial technology utilization. Technology owners who hold a proprietary position today through a limited monopoly granted by the patent system or trade secret protection are not guaranteed to reap the economic benefits of the commercial uses of their technology. The technology asset, as I envision it, really is the starting point in the race to attain early market entry and market dominance.

Physical infrastructure is the third building block in a national innovation system. This includes everything from the quality, sophistication, and ease of transportation systems to the constructed environment in the broadest sense.

Since leaving the government, I have had the opportunity in the last few years to do some technology work in the former Soviet Union. I think we all remember the days when you could visit Moscow and not see any cars. It is now virtually impossible to get to a meeting on time in Moscow unless you budget an hour-and-a-half to get to your appointment. This is true in places like Bangkok as well. Therefore, if you are trying to conduct any sort of business, the physical transportation infrastructure is absolutely critical to efficiency. Transportation systems are going to be profoundly driven by the use and deployment of advanced technology, like the intelligent vehicle highway system (IVHS). The smart systems that are being demonstrated right now in test beds in various parts of the country will not only afford the United States leadership in terms of new products and services we can deploy and new markets we can tap, but also in terms of tremendously enhancing our own environment for conducting business.

A nation's capital formation and allocation system are absolutely critical for innovation. This is the most important building block we have to deal with right now. In order to remain competitive, firms must acquire capital to pay for innovation, production, capacity, and global marketing. Businesses and government share certain concerns, but they do not agree on the ways and means of achieving the optimal system for capital formation and allocation. Indeed, some economists now say the United States has an innovation-hostile capital formation and allocation system. It is not that we do not have lots of capital. We have billions of dollars in capital. The problems are where the capital goes, for what purposes, and what results it gives to the society at large and business in particular. I will explain this in more detail.

The next building block is the regulatory framework. I would rank the existing framework with the current capital formation and allocation system as a profound disincentive to our ability to have a world-class national innovation system. The regulatory environment in which firms operate at home and abroad heavily influences their decision-making. This covers everything from the types of business protection, or lack of it, to intellectual property rights and product liability. Competition policy, better known as antitrust policy, and directives often regulate what a firm may develop at home and abroad. The set of laws and complex regulations embedded in the government procurement and acquisition system currently regulate private sector suppliers to the government. I am sure many of you are familiar with that morass.

Indeed, there are many major U.S. firms that will not even participate with government customers because of the problems associated with the acquisition system. For example, Motorola chose not to supply the government with mobile radios during Desert Storm because they had to guarantee, as one of the regulations in the acquisition system, that nowhere else in the world were mobile radios being sold for a penny less than the Department of Defense was paying. Motorola obviously could not guarantee that. So where did we procure our mobile radios? Japan.

The international trading system is a critical enabling factor for national innovation. A firm's early entry into and penetration of key global markets is determined by its ability to participate fully and equitably in the global trading system and, in parallel, to obtain relief from trading systems that subsidize or protect infant or targeted industries, that force mandatory cross-licensing or technology transfers, or that commit a host of other anti-trade sins.

When I was in the White House Office of Science and Technology Policy during the Reagan administration, I was on the periphery of the famous Kansai Airport negotiation with Japan because I was working on a lot of Japanese-related technology trade issues. The Japanese fought against doing anything to provide transparency in the bidding process for our construction companies. I have not followed the issue since, but somebody told me that the United States is not a player in that process, in spite of a trade agreement, because of a whole set of non-transparent cultural issues that have worked collectively to keep us out of that market. I would add that the Three Gorges Project is another example of a project in which U.S. companies have not been able to participate because our own government has not being willing to put our firms on an equal footing with foreign competitors by giving them access to the Export-Import Bank and supporting them in other ways.

Reciprocal access to international investment opportunities is another building block in a national innovation system. The international economy and the globalization of R&D, finance, and manufacturing currently offer firms investment opportunities abroad. Nations that do not adopt reciprocity in international investment flows are really creating an entry barrier to their home markets. For example, if you compare the direct foreign investment figures of both the United States and Europe vis-à-vis Japan, you would be shocked. Per capita, there is almost no American direct foreign investment in Japan.

American firms do not really have the opportunity to invest in and acquire Japanese assets. Even in the more sensational cases where investors and companies have acquired majority ownership of shares in Japanese firms, they have not been able to exercise any corporate governance because of informal barriers. On the other hand, the United States and Europe have a fairly open reciprocal international investment flow and can participate in each other's economies.

The industrial structure for innovation is another key factor. This is a very important point. The industrial structure in which a firm conducts its primary innovation activities has a profound effect on time to market and market penetration. Today in the United States we have a very interesting situation. Many of our most advanced technology assets are developed or incubated in fragile, capital-starved entrepreneurial firms that are vulnerable to premature failure—particularly if a company is in a small or scattered industry or in a new industry, in which the ability to share information, costs, and risks are limited.

On the other hand, if you look at technology that is incubated in or through partnerships with larger, more vertically integrated industries, you often see some very innovative things occurring where producers and end users across multiple applications pool their resources and risks to develop and commercialize technology.

Let me give an example from the construction industry. The construction industry obviously has a tremendous need for the most advanced flexible materials. These types of materials are being developed in the aerospace industry, in the auto industry, in our national laboratories for defense purposes, and by sporting goods manufacturers. You could envision a case of a number of vertically integrated teams with players from all of those industrial sectors who have a common interest in, say, developing or using advanced ceramics. They would not have any antitrust problems. They would not be concerned about pooling their crown jewels because they are in different business lines. But they could have a way to get to the market faster and more quickly with cost-effective products through those synergies and links, than if they tried to team up with their direct competitors in a traditional horizontal consortium.

In a horizontal consortium, competitors rarely share critical information. They help each other get to a common point, and then they go off and compete. In a vertical teaming relationship, they can share their proprietary crown jewels. If you look at the strategies used by some of our foreign competitors who get to the market in many industries on a cycle time much faster than U.S. firms, you find that they are pooling and sharing risks and costs across industrial sectors and multiple product lines.

Business management and manufacturing practices also profoundly affect innovation. As you know, in this country we pioneered what is known as the Tailoris Mass-Production System. We also pioneered many of the current management practices that are increasingly viewed as hindrances and disincentives to early market entry and penetration. Horizontal, cross-functional teaming relationships are increasingly replacing rigid, hierarchical, or inflexible organizational structures. The Malcolm Baldridge Quality Awards have played a big role in helping change cultures of firms that need relationships among their supplier networks. In the traditional, hostile relationship, firms go out every year and rebid their supplier network rather than working with them to upgrade their capability, and vice versa. And the whole new world of virtual manufacturing, or integrated computer manufacturing, is having a profound effect on U.S. firms. I had the pleasure last year of visiting Motorola's new manufacturing facility in Phoenix, which produces satellites for the Iridium communications network. Experts consider this manufacturing facility one of the most advanced. Rather than building each satellite from the ground up, they have a system in which the satellites are all built concurrently.

The Japanese deserve tremendous credit for pioneering and utilizing many of the most advanced manufacturing techniques. This also relates to how they treat their workers and labor. They do not have the hostile management/labor relations we have in the United States. To many of us working in the competitiveness arena, the greatest obstacles to the involvement of workers in management decisions are the traditional labor unions because participation takes away from their power structure. The National Labor Relations Board has had suits brought by labor unions. For instance, a big labor union brought a suit against DuPont for having self-managed work teams in the factory because they eliminated labor shop stewards.

All of these factors comprise a holistic national innovation system. Evidently, nations provide the primary staging platforms for commercial innovation. Collectively, we need to look at the system of incentives and impediments for each of these factors and decide what we can do as a country to create incentives and break down disincentives. We need to optimize our system for the next century, which requires us to create wealth and skilled jobs here in the United States based on our leadership in science and technology and our skilled human resource base.

I believe that the United States is at a turning point. If we do not begin to develop both a national innovation system and a systemic approach, our leadership in science and technology is going to create more accessible raw material for our foreign competitors to use. I will share with you an anecdote on that.

I was involved very intensely in the late 1980s and early 1990s with the Japanese on technology issues. They used to refer to our universities as their raw material suppliers. They saw our universities as creating the knowledge and technology assets that they converted into products and sold back to us. We were negotiating a very difficult intelligent manufacturing systems initiative. One of the Japanese negotiators from MITI said the following to me, and he really sort of let the cat out of the bag, which we already knew. However you structure this, he said, as long as this is an R&D project, we are going to clean your clocks because you do not have the capacity to take this and get it to market ahead of us. So we want all these programs to be R&D oriented. We want access to your knowledge, creativity, people, and institutions. We will take that back and deploy it through our system, which has a better capital formation process that does not impede our businesses through regulatory problems. Every single trade regulation or trade policy is geared to support and help Japanese manufacturing entities at home and abroad. With our management business structures, we do not waste time on management labor problems. We do things collectively. So, go ahead, focus all our projects on R&D. We will contribute a little money, but we are going to be the ones who produce the product and services that come out of it.

I will throw in a political comment here regarding the government not supporting grants to companies to create more commercial industrial technology. I would say that unless the federal government and Congress begin to deal with capital formation and allocation and clean up the regulatory mess, we will just be creating more raw material for our competitors.

FINANCING INNOVATION

What should we do about the financing environment for innovation? Banks and venture capital firms no longer play a role. The reason for that, again, is regulatory, compounded by culture.

At one time in our country, banks played a major role. Then in 1933, we passed the Glass-Steagall law in the aftermath of the Depression and the stock market crash. This law makes it illegal for banks to own shares of industrial enterprises or to be involved in security underwriting. Therefore, banks play no role in what many believe to be the most critical phase of technology incubation and financing through equity participation. They are only involved in debt financing of major corporations.

Venture capital firms played a very important role back in the 1970s and 1980s in the creation of Silicon Valley, the semiconductor and biotech industries. Their role is increasingly changed now. They no longer invest in seed or early stage financing because the growth potential of their investment is very uncertain. It is too hard to predict the outcome to justify the risks. They really want a very clearly defined exit strategy, and they are really only looking at a three-year to five-year window. Start-up companies do not want to go to the venture capital list unless they are absolutely desperate. Venture capital firms will take all your equity, put in a management team, and keep you on starvation rations because they have to manage for the fact that out of their investment portfolio only 30 percent of their ventures have any chance of success. So they take huge returns from that 30 percent to balance the 70 percent that fail.

What should we do? We clearly need to redirect capital allocation through tax reform. You have read about flat taxes. Moving from a consumption-oriented tax system to a savings-oriented tax system is something most policy groups that have been looking at tax reform advocate. It is a question of what the transition is. Let me just mention a couple of things that, collectively, could make a profound difference. The R&E tax credit has been a primary incentive for increasing corporate investment in R&D. However, it has never been made permanent, and the credit base structure has made it applicable only to a few firms. So one important recommendation is to make that tax credit permanent, so every year you know that you will be able to take advantage of it. Then change the base so everybody, as opposed to only a few companies, is eligible for the R&E credit.

Another interesting idea is to provide a 20 percent credit to encourage collaborative R&D ventures in the United States. I talked earlier about the need for pooling and teaming. The tax system could be a neutral way to encourage that, as opposed to giving direct grant subsidies to individual firms. What is nice about doing a lot of these incentives through the tax system is that everyone would be eligible. With direct subsidies of specific firms, even if you pour $10 billion into grant programs for commercial technology development, there would still be a lot of companies that would not get them. And where do you draw the line on the government's role in terms of picking up the risks and rewards of private sector innovation? It is much cleaner, neater, fairer, and more comprehensive to do these things through the tax system and concentrate our tax resources on creating a broad infrastructure and base of knowledge through basic and strategic research that is mission-driven.

It is also incredible that at this stage of our history we are still dealing with a capital gains tax. We are the only advanced industrial country in the world with a punitive capital gains tax structure. Everybody else—the Europeans, the Japanese—has gotten rid of this structure. We have allowed ourselves to treat this as a rich/poor issue. All the facts and statistics show that this is not the case. The idea that a reduction in the capital gains tax would reward the rich is a political canard. Every business study says the one thing they would like is to reduce the capital gains tax. What we have now is double taxation. You pay at both the individual and the corporate level, and this is a huge disincentive for investment. It favors debt bias over equity in our tax code. You can deduct debt from your taxes, but you cannot take advantage of equity. Equity investments drive growth. Thus, we need to eliminate the double taxation of individual and corporate investment income in order to increase the availability of investment capital and reduce costs.

We also have a treasury regulation that provides a complete incentive for our companies to do their R&D overseas. We could change this with an Executive Order (the Bush and Clinton administrations have tried). I think Wall Street is protecting itself and not looking at the good of the country. The regulation is fairly detailed and complex but is in the tax code. If you want to get tax benefits from R&D, you must do it overseas. Now, do we want to have our R&D done overseas, away from our platform of innovation? No. So we should get rid of that treasury regulation. It will cost a little bit of money, but the benefits for productivity will be huge. We should also get rid of Glass-Steagall. It is obsolete, and we need all of our financing sources participating in innovation.

REGULATORY OBSTACLES

In regard to regulatory structures, I want to mention a few quick items. The regulatory framework is really a case of huge national resources going into something that has nothing to do with productivity. Let me give you some statistics collected by the National Association of Manufacturers in a wonderful little booklet describing what manufacturing means to the American economy. U.S. firms spend about $65 billion responding to government environmental regulations. They spend another $55 billion responding to health-related regulations and $55 billion on legal services. The statistic mentioned earlier, that we spend approximately $170 billion collectively on R&D, represents money that goes into productivity. The rest does nothing to add to our wealth or create jobs.

Clearly, we want regulations to protect our families, ourselves, and society at large. The issue is balance. Most experts on the regulatory regime think we have gone too far and allowed regulation to become a disincentive. I will share with you just one area where regulation is now very negative— product liability. The product liability system varies from state to state. It has neither rhyme nor reason and is driven by the Trial Lawyers Association. Awards given to plaintiffs have no caps, and this is a nightmare. In terms of its impact on innovation, I will refer you to the literature. In fact, the National Research Council (NRC) did one of the best studies on product liability reform and its relationship to innovation.

DuPont used to be a major material supplier of medical devices. When you want to have access at some point in your life to certain types of medical devices, the United States may no longer manufacture medical devices (within the next 10 to 20 years). As a result of the product liability system, even if a manufacturer's materials had nothing to do with the cause of an injury, and even if the materials they sold to an end-use manufacturer were totally modified by that end-use manufacturer, the manufacturer can still be held totally liable. Because awards have no caps, a company could be wiped out. DuPont said, "Why should we do that?"

So here we have the quandary of our government spending lots of money on R&D in advanced materials for, among other reasons, medical application. And yet we do not have any companies that are going to commercialize the applications because of product liability laws. So who is going to benefit from that taxpayer investment in the new materials that lead to a whole new generation of products? We will not. I am giving you that as an example of how these issues are linked. You cannot look at one in isolation from the others.

Antitrust is also a very important issue, but when the laws and regulations were originally set up, antitrust legislation had a different purpose than it has now. We still have an antitrust system with a philosophical basis from the 1920s, when we were concerned about competition between Ohio and Indiana, not competition between the United States and a global environment.

The Justice Department, as we speak, has issued "Antitrust Guidelines and Innovation Policy." In a nutshell, first they look at the type of R&D a firm does. If a firm conducts R&D that could lead to something that could keep another company out of a market, the Department of Justice will initiate antitrust action. That is anti-competitive behavior. I always thought that doing R&D was to give a firm an advantage over competitors—that was one of the reasons you invested in it. So we have moved antitrust way upstream.

Look at the implications of this for new industries, such as those emerging around the national information infrastructure. You see in the announced mergers and acquisitions of companies a reorganization that will alter the current industrial structure, but it will not take you to this national information infrastructure. AT&T is divesting. Cable computer telecommunication companies are reorganizing in order to get the bits and pieces they need to participate in whatever this new industry is going to be, both in manufactured products and in the software and service end. Yet the Justice Department is looking at all of those potential acquisitions and mergers from a traditional 1920s antitrust perspective.

Similarly, whatever you think about Microsoft, whether they are the thousand-pound gorilla or not, as an American citizen I was very upset that our government went, on its own, to the European Community Commission, to the gentleman in charge of antitrust policy, to initiate talks about how Microsoft should be busted up in Europe. Why do we want to bust up one of our leading companies in Europe? I do not know. Microsoft is one of the few companies, an exception to all the losses we accrue from intellectual property, from which we are getting a lot of money back.

Antitrust is a critical issue relating to innovation. Our foreign competitors have totally different policies. The Japanese have never brought an antitrust suit against a Japanese company, ever.

ROLE OF THE NATIONAL LABORATORIES

The construction industry is a user of technologies developed by others. That is not necessarily bad as long as they are involved up front with the producers of their innovation stream. I think one of the ways to move quickly but still avoid antitrust concerns is to catalyze some vertically integrated teaming relationships on both the producer and the user side. You are not going to be threatened by people who make certain types of sporting equipment, and you are going to have a lot of needs in information technologies, too, managing inventory and all of that.

One thing that I would recommend to this industry is that they go to the national laboratories and take the time and effort to see what they have. There is no question that the laboratories are developing a lot of things of tremendous value to this industry. The construction industries could get in on the ground floor—maybe in some of the consortia that are formed—and participate in a way that gives them some proprietary capabilities to move forward. I am sure there are trade associations in this industry that I am not knowledgeable about, but they could put together a lot of structures to get together with the federal laboratories and also the universities. Cutting across the industrial sector is an innovative way to do this.

When I was in the Commerce Department, we found out about the intelligent vehicle highway system initiative (IVHS). This was a classic example of government operation. The Department of Transportation was acting in isolation. I reached out to Transportation and the R&D people, and we did some interagency work on it. But in that project there was going to be a tremendous need for advanced displays, and the flat panel display industry is so important as an enabling technology in the chain. Since the IVHS was a government mission, we suggested building in a procurement need to stimulate our fragile entrepreneurial advance display manufacturers, but Transportation turned their backs on that. So all the displays that are being used are from Japan, which to me was upsetting, unnecessary, and counterproductive.

If you look at things as part of a system as opposed to looking at each piece in isolation, you begin to see where you can fit things in and how they are related. I give the Japanese real credit for doing that in almost everything they do.

The Council on Competitiveness has not looked at the movement of goods from city to city in a coherent way. Some companies, as I recall, Frito-Lay, Inc., won the Malcolm Baldridge Award for an incredibly sophisticated transportation movement and inventory system that uses technologies in a service sense. I think that this board in the NRC (BICE) could make a tremendous contribution by looking at that kind of issue and getting a study out on it.

I could tell you that Los Alamos National Laboratory, where I am on the board, has a very innovative initiative in the transportation arena with the Department of Transportation. They are looking at the whole traffic control system in Albuquerque as a test bed. Detractors question why a weapons laboratory is interested in transportation. Los Alamos makes, designs, and manages the nuclear weapons process, but they also bring to the table advanced computational simulation capability, which is unique and can help our economy. They are working with a number of major construction firms. The board might want to take a team out to look at that because they are doing a lot in transportation.

CONCLUSION

In conclusion, these are the points I have tried to make this morning. You can have a tremendous human resource base, and we need to work on that. You can be the leader in science and technology. You can be at the forefront of developing every new innovative technology that is going to drive new product services and create whole new industries. But if you do not embed those assets in an innovation environment that provides incentives for getting products and services to the market quickly in terms of quality, price, and market penetration, all of this will be for naught. What we need to do, what we can do, is be the staging platform for world leadership in science and technology and its utilization.

Future of Infrastructure Finance

Bruce D. McDowell
Government Policy Research
Advisory Commission on Intergovernmental Relations

I used to give speeches called "How to Improve Public Works with No New Money." They were very creative speeches. But the kind of speech you have to give now is, "Public Works Improvements with even Less Money Than You Thought You Had."

Fellow panel chair Nancy Rutledge Connery and I worked together on the National Council on Public Works Improvement. The problem with the council's report was that it came out right at the end of the Reagan administration and was passed along to a new administration, which, for one reason or another, did not pick it up. President Clinton gave it a whirl with his investment program, and it went down in flames. It was not quite the right time, but the right time is coming.

I had the task at the Advisory Commission on Intergovernmental Relations of bringing together people intergovernmentally and across the agencies of government to discuss what a federal infrastructure strategy should look like. One task force looked at how you do finance in constrained situations. The basic conclusion was that in any kind of infrastructure planning you need a financial planning element from the very beginning. We published the results in November 1993 as, "High Performance Public Works: A New Federal Infrastructure Investment Strategy for America."

We see an example of this financial planning now in the Intermodal Surface Transportation Efficiency Act (ISTEA), which requires that all transportation plans at the state and metropolitan level be done in a financially constrained fashion. State and metropolitan planning organizations are beginning to hire financial analysts to get the job done along with the rest of the planning process. Our four panelists will offer observations on how financing is affecting the provision of infrastructure today and how it will continue to do so in the future.

67

Dulles Greenway: Private Provision of Transportation Infrastructure

Charles E. Williams, Major General (retired)
Rebuild Incorporated

I feel very fortunate to be standing here, not only for those who sponsored the Dulles Greenway but also for our nation, the state of Virginia, and everyone included in this colloquium because the Dulles Greenway is the first of its kind in more than 100 years in Virginia. I do not know how that shakes out around the country, but it has been a long time since we have had a completely delivered, privately owned toll road.

The story of the Dulles Greenway is a very long one, and I will spare you the story prior to my arrival. September 29, 1993, is the day we broke ground. The Dulles Toll Road runs about 13 miles from the Beltway, I-495 west to Dulles airport. The road we just opened, called the Dulles Greenway, is 14.1 miles long, going from the Dulles airport west to the historical town of Leesburg, Virginia.

One of the things we learned early on about a successful toll road is that the road has to leave one rather significant point and connect to another one. In our case, it leaves from Dulles airport, which is the airport with the greatest capacity to expand on the East Coast and has a $2 billion capital program ongoing. So it made a lot of strategic sense to connect a road to that significant facility. Beyond that, the Dulles area is a dynamic area for a lot of reasons. The Air and Space Museum is moving to that vicinity, so this also factored into some of the corporate thinking. We connect to Leesburg, which has historical significance and is growing. That was, overall, the fundamental strategy that went into the corporate planning on selecting the location for the road.

There was already a public need for an infrastructure facility of this type. Let us look at a couple of reasons. Number one, we needed to unload traffic off the lateral north roadway, which is Route 7, and the southern lateral of Route 50 and Interstate 66. At the same time, that particular portion of the county offered the best opportunity for growth because in and around the Washington area the other corridors are approaching maximum development. Therefore, the Dulles corridor seemed to offer the best opportunity, as economists were telling us at the time. The strategy for locating the road on this footprint was two-pronged. One, it made good strategic sense from a planning standpoint. And two, it connected well to the economic growth pattern in that corridor. The point is, you do not locate a toll road, or any other facility to which you expect to have user fees attached, just any place. You must really think it through, not only in order to make good transportation and public sense, but also to match the economics.

There are two questions I think are very important, one for the public side and one for the private. We have really got to think about where we are going to be in the year 2020, and that is why this forum today is so important. The NRC is out front on the thought process. We have to think about the whole infrastructure question as it relates to transportation in the year 2020, because we simply cannot put facilities in place overnight. Delivery of private facilities is very difficult because they are linked to private financing. However, whether the financing comes from the public or private sector, it is still a very difficult business.

Virginia is very fortunate because a lot of money flows into its transportation coffers. The problem is that some of the $2 billion, in my opinion, is going into the wrong pots. For example, 45 percent of the transportation dollars are going toward new construction; that should be 75 percent, to my way of thinking. Therefore, the 40 percent going to maintenance, which drains the new dollars, quite frankly is too high. On the other hand, Virginia has a lot of transportation network that is obsolete and needs a tremendous amount of maintenance.

The way for the private sector to become a partner is to carve into the maintenance area with new construction and help reduce it to 20 percent, where, I believe, it should be. Then the private sector could take a whack at the inefficiencies in the 15 percent in operations by putting in smart highway operating techniques and reduce that to about 5 percent. Really, the transportation dollar should be broken out as 5 percent operations, 20 percent maintenance, and 75 percent new construction, if you were proportioned somewhat nearer the ideal.

Virginia has a lot of highways and as a result a big maintenance problem. The state will be spending $40 billion over the next 20 years. Virginia would still be unable to fulfill its total maintenance requirements. This is what drives the whole notion of enticing the private sector to come in and help with the problem because, regardless of which side of the aisle may be driving the political process, you cannot handle this $40 billion problem in the next 20 years without help. This is also why there are very good opportunities in the state of Virginia for private sector infrastructure projects.

These were some of the high hurdles that we had to get over. Securing equity sponsors was a big issue because, obviously, that was the first dollar spent, that was the high risk dollar. Equity sponsors are not easy to find because you are talking about soliciting an individual, a pension fund, a bank, or some financial institution to put money at risk and receive a no-book earning for quite some years. So, quite frankly, the sponsors are very selective. There are some out there, but you have to be very mindful that they are not easy to capture.

Local and state agreements are also very important. Environmental work, in my estimation, is at the top of the list of hurdles. You simply cannot finesse the environmental process. You operate with a deregulated mentality, but at the same time there are certain compliances that you must do because the whole concept of privatization is that you are borrowing a project from the public portfolio and moving it over into the private world for a period of time. You will privatize it, operate it like a private entity for a certain concession period, and then it goes back to the public. The responsible public entity, be it a state or a city or whatever, is the ultimate owner of that facility, so you cannot ever step completely away from the public arena.

Securing permits and engineering are self-explanatory, but it was very important to get the right contractor and that the contractor listen to the new drumbeat. Securing the financing was very difficult. Our project costs were about $326 million using three different types of money: a heavy equity slice; some construction-dollar funding, which we call short-term money; and some 30-year money, which obviously was of the long-term debt type. In addition to getting the sponsors, we had to cross two additional hurdles, to find a consortium of banks that would provide the short-term financing and long-term lenders who could stay the course for 30 years.

The endgame was simple. No one wants traffic tie ups, and no one wants more taxes. The only other option was tolls. We do not make any excuse for the toll rate because we are creating an option for the traveling public, not a demand. We have given people an alternative that is a "quality of life" enhancement. If time is important to the motorist, that must be factored into the decision to pay the toll.

In our case, there are parallel arteries running east and west of our roadway that will carry the traveling public from western Virginia and West Virginia into the Washington area, but they have more than 20 traffic lights. The model travel time on either of those arteries is about 1 hour and 15 minutes from Leesburg to Constitution Avenue in downtown D.C., varying about five minutes depending on whether you are coming from north or south. The model time for the Greenway now is about 40 minutes to Washington, D.C. The real issue is whether you want to pay to save time or you would like to stay on the other arteries and fight the traffic.

This project, as I mentioned, was the first of its kind. It was fast paced and very expensive because we probably have a heavier slice of equity than we would like to see going forward. Because this was a pioneering effort, there were a lot of skeptics who questioned whether the concept was going to work; therefore, the equity requirements were a little bit higher.

There has been a lot of social/economic fallout over this project. We created more than 500 jobs in the region very quickly and quietly. You do not normally think of a privatization effort doing this sort of thing. We were able to attract blue chip lenders, the top of the line in terms of long-term lenders. This obviously made control and management critical. The schedule had to be made, and, of course, the public used this first project as an outdoor theater because it was something that they had not seen for some time.

We had everything that you could possibly have here in the way of challenges. We had to acquire the right of way for 14 miles. We had no condemnation authority per se. Not one acre, not one inch was condemned by the state. We actually purchased outright a third of the road from 47 different landowners, with individual negotiations to get a 250-foot swath across their property. The other third of the property right of way was obtained through a mutual type conveyance arrangement. The landowner was interested in developing, say, a large residential area, and it was convenient to have a road and an interchange at that location. In exchange for that, the landowner conveyed a portion of the property.

The eastern portion was on federal property. You cannot purchase federal property; you have to work out some other arrangement. We have a very long leasehold arrangement with the Metropolitan Washington Airport Authority, whereby we leased the 226-acre swath that we touched. In this part of the roadway, we impacted 64 acres of wetlands, so another critical job was to mitigate for the environmental impact. With the wetlands site, we had all of the problems of "not in my backyard." The regulatory process required us to do a two-for-one mitigation. We had to put in place about 126 acres with an assortment of plants and trees. The handling of the planting was very delicate. We increased that to 150 acres because, once we started looking at it, there were some enhancements required to make the site a truly class act. So we made it into an environmental show piece. It is being considered for use now by one of the major universities for science work and other conservation training. So these were the by-products.

I just want to mention one thing here about the general contractor and the way we worked this. All of you who have dealt with construction know about "retainage." Retainage is normally a portion or percent of the monthly draw that the owner holds for contingencies down the way. One of the innovative spins we put on our deal was that we took the retainage up front from the contractor, and we took it from a source that was not cash. We took a letter of credit. So, during the execution we held a letter of credit from our contractor rather than retaining his cash. This was perceived as an incentive for the contractor because, if the contractor intended to do the job right in the first place, and the cash that was expected was not tampered with, this was obviously better for the company as a hold. This also put us in a better posture with the financing institution because we had our retainage up front. So when the project was presented to the financing institutions, we were able to show the letter of credit to answer the question of how to deal with some of the contingencies.

I think it was also important to manage peripheral talk normally facing the highway contractor. The traditional picture a contractor would normally be faced with is—build 14 miles of road, so many bridges, etc., and, oh, by the way, would be asked to do all of these other things as well, relocate the utilities, work the insurance out, do the wetlands, and handle the regulatory agencies. We had 176 permits associated with this project, which the contractor would have had to deal with. We worked with 17 regulatory bodies of different sorts—federal, state, county, and town—as well as other interested groups. What we did as the owner was to take all of the risk associated with this collateral work and manage those tasks ourselves. Now the contractor had a clear shot at the project. He had just the roadway to deal with. All of the tasks that would have created problems were pretty dismissed away for the contractor because the owner took those.

And then, of course, the last challenge is the organization of the team. Across the board, I might be the only person who has fully developed a project of this type from inception all the way through delivery. The Dulles Greenway was opened on its 24-month anniversary to the hour. We broke ground September 29, 1993, at 11 a.m., and we cut the ribbon September 29, 1995, at 11 a.m. It was six months ahead of schedule, and obviously that early completion potential was an incentive for the contractor.

DISCUSSION

A question was raised regarding operations and maintenance and whether that will also be privately funded. In the operation and maintenance section of the financing plan, we have reserves for overlay pavement. So the money is already in the financials. As to whether the private sector will be more efficient at maintaining highways, we are providing data on that very quickly now in an empirical way. I think even the state of Virginia will say, after a period of time, that the techniques we used to put the facility in place will most likely reduce the maintenance requirements.

I will give you an example of some of the things we did. As most people who build these facilities know, there is a range of what you can do in compliance with specifications. We operated at the very top end of the specifications. For example, our roadbed required 12 inches of stone before the asphalt. We treated the second 6 inches with cement to make it stronger. We were within specification without cement, but we chose to treat it with cement. We know this will have a lasting effect and reduce the maintenance.

We have funding in our financial pro forma to overlay the road every seven years. We are hoping to get close to 10 years between repavings. We have a pavement-monitoring system whereby we do a lot of diagnostic work. So we will be getting a lot of intelligence about what is happening as we go along. That is how the maintenance will be reduced.

The Greenway has no public money at all. It is unique. It was not a public/private venture as you know it, where we had a portion of federal money and some matching amount from the state. This was all private money. I would maintain that this is not the way to do it, but we had to do it this way in order to break the first one through.

The Intermodal Surface Transportation Efficiency Act (ISTEA) came along about midway through our development. We were not able to utilize it, but we are clearly looking to it in the future. In a model sense, the way it should work would be through the flexibility ISTEA legislation creates for the states. The state of Virginia, hypothetically, would have to petition the federal government to allow certain allocated funding to Virginia to be used for a private venture. That is the way the ISTEA works, as I understand it. ISTEA comes with no money. This was a misnomer when it was suggested. When the bill passed, everybody went with their hands out saying, "Where's the money?" There was no new money.

The same amount of money flows into the states. It is just that they have more flexibility on what to do with it. If the secretary of transportation (through the governing bodies) elects not to put the money on maintenance but on something new, the ISTEA legislation would allow him to switch it in those different trenches and then work with the private sector to get the project done. Our road did not have any ISTEA money.

A reasonable question to ask is, when you turn this roadway back to the public, what do you get from the public? The public contribution was to pass legislation to allow the private sector to do this. The Virginia constitution prohibited the state's good faith and credit from being involved in a private arrangement. They entered with us into something called a comprehensive agreement for handling this project. There were no guarantees for anything. But if, for some reason, we would have faltered along the way and could not have completed the roadway, the public would not have been left with a white elephant. The state had the option to come in and take over.

Virginia did not put in any funding, guarantees, or loans. The right model of this would have had the state make a contribution, but we were facing so many hurdles at the time—breaking paradigms in terms of legislation, moving a very sluggish assembly of politicians from a center in which they had operated for years—it was probably, in defense of Virginia, just too much to ask at the time. The state has since followed through with some super legislation and has been superb to work with. Today, probably, Virginia has the best enabling legislation for public/private ventures in the country. They can now make guarantee-an in kind-type contributions.

Another question for Virginia was how the state ensures that it is not going to take title to a roadway with huge maintenance requirements after our concession period of 40 years? They are protected through this comprehensive agreement. We must maintain and operate this facility at no less than the state standards. So, at a minimum we will be giving them back what they would have had if they had maintained it. And to make sure that happens, they had inspectors out with us during the construction and also during the operation to make certain the standards are met.

In trying to extend the maintenance period from every 7 to every 11 years, we are not deferring required maintenance. To meet the requirement for a roadway of this nature, built to our design, the state expects an overlay to the pavement every seven years. We provided for that. We will have a pavement monitoring system in place during operation to tell us what is going on. We will not overlay unless there is a reason to overlay, so we will be prepared about the sixth year to petition the state and say, "Based on all of the data we have collected, it does not make sense for us to do this. Don't you agree?"

Regarding the toll rate, there are two relevant government bodies in the state of Virginia, the State Corporation Commission, which regulates rates, and the Commonwealth Transportation Board, which regulates policy. These bodies are the arms for the governor, and they made decisions for us. The Commonwealth Transportation Board decided how the roadway would be managed, designed, and operated, which are policy issues.

Setting the toll rate was a joint decision between the private entity, us, and the State Corporation Commission, and it was negotiated. We had a certain project cost. Obviously the investors, the sponsors, needed an acceptable rate of return because of the front-end risk. A combination of this rate of return, servicing the debt, and operating the road is what set the tolls. We did not break out our funding by task. We had short-term money, which we needed to get the road built, which we have just completed. That amount of funding was provided mostly by a consortium of banks. They have limits, as you know, on the number of years they can loan money. The long-term debt financing was done by another group of financial institutions, like insurance companies, pension funds, etc.

The initial dollars came from the sponsors. These were the people and the entities who own the toll road. The very first dollars committed to the project are the equity dollars, then the bank dollars, and later the long-term lending dollars. There is an agreed upon cap on the rate of return with the state of Virginia. If the cap is ever reached, the surplus goes into a special account, and we will negotiate about how we deal with that surplus.

In summary, all players, lenders, regulators, owners, contractors, and consultants did a fantastic job on this pioneering effort and should be given proper credit. I was very fortunate to have the opportunity to manage the execution of the project.

Flexibility in Infrastructure Finance

Richard Mudge
Apogee Research

We are all in the business of trying to make sense out of words that are so vague they probably have little meaning to most people, the word "infrastructure," for example. Sometimes we think we are going to define it better and call it "public works infrastructure," which probably means very little to most people. Another great word is "privatization," or its refined definition, "public/private partnerships," but it is still the same nebulous thing. My current favorite is "innovative finance" because it makes things sound free. Recently, however, some reality has begun to appear as some actual projects have been created out of innovative financing and privatization—the Dulles Greenway, for example.

To show my bias as an economist, I believe that an understanding of finance begins with economics. Economics should tell us why we care about public works. In very simple terms, infrastructure provides two types of benefits. The first is direct benefits. These are things like travel time savings, clean water, and reduced vehicle operating costs. These are very important because they represent goods or services for which people should be willing to pay. In other words, the financial success of any business, whether public or private, depends on having a potential source of direct revenue attached to it. The second type of benefit is more indirect, to users and non-users alike. These involve market access, productivity, and health and safety benefits. I believe that this second category is an order of magnitude larger than the first.

Apogee Research has just finished a series of studies that started with the Corps of Engineers and passed on to the Federal Highway Administration (FHWA). In this case, since FHWA supported the work, we examined the role of highways in supporting economic growth. Our studies showed that highway investment allows private firms to make more efficient use of their capital, labor, and raw materials. If you translate these efficiency gains into an annual rate of return, for the last 40 years the nation's investment in highway capital has provided benefits equivalent to a return to private industry of about 25 to 30 percent a year.

The results also showed that the larger the network, the larger the returns. In other words, thinking small is not good for the economy. This finding reminds us why public works are public. The large indirect benefits can be called "public goods," but they are benefits a private firm cannot capture. So when we think about privatizing public works, a key success factor is ensuring that the public sector retains a leading role.

Success in financing projects requires two things: cash, or more correctly, a cash flow, and a financial mechanism. The former can be user fees, dedicated taxes, whatever. In many ways, this is the easier of the two to find. The financial mechanism represents a tool for translating the flow of funds into a real project. Again, I apologize for using examples from transportation, but that happens to be the field I know best.

Within transportation, the key financial mechanism for the last 40 years has been the Highway Trust Fund. The primary financial cash flow for that has been the federal motor fuel tax. The Highway Trust Fund has been very successful. Although it was designed to build the Interstate Highway System, it has also become something on which to hang all the planning and policy work at the national level and, especially, at the state level. It has been a focal point that helps organize planners and engineers. In other words, its success is measured well beyond the financial tool it was designed to be.

The Highway Trust Fund has been broken, however, for at least the last 20 years. In the early 1970s, the Interstate Highway System was basically complete. For the last 20 years, transportation has been searching for an alternative financial mechanism. Three financial options occur to me. The first option is to keep the Highway Trust Fund. It is not necessarily a bad mechanism as long as you put more money into it. The only time that happened on any significant scale was in 1982 when Congress passed a nickel tax increase that went into the Highway Trust Fund. The problem is the lack of motivation. The need to increase funding has been backed up by "needs" studies that show shortfalls in spending of $1 trillion, $2 trillion, $3 trillion, or more. The scale is hard for most people to relate to. Also, it is hard to draw an economic link showing that if we spent all that money, the world would be a better place. Basically, I think this "needs" oriented, more of the same, approach has failed. You can call that strike one.

Another approach is privatization. This is not a new idea. The state of Virginia in the nineteenth century had a policy of matching 50/50 any private firm that wanted to build a railroad, canal, or toll road. The state of Virginia still owns part of the railroad between Richmond and Washington, D.C., because of that.

In the 1980s, President Reagan came in, and there was renewed interest in what the private sector could do, but there were very few successes. Greenway is a success because it is open, but, as General Williams said, it is not something they would do again. State Route 91 is about to open in California in December 1995. This is a high occupancy vehicle lane that will use market-based pricing. They have the authority to change the tolls up to 24 times a day based on the amount of traffic. I cannot imagine it not being a huge success. It was also a painful process and took a long time to implement. There are other examples. In wastewater treatment, there are a growing number of privatized facilities. But overall, there have been many more failures than successes. I would call that strike two.

The third option is to develop a new public financial mechanism. After all, we talk about reinventing government, and there must be new things that can be done. Many of them are already there on paper. The Intermodal Surface Transportation Efficiency Act (ISTEA) was passed in 1991. It contains a lot of imaginative financial tools. Section 1012, my favorite number, offers a tremendous number of good things. For example, it allows public soft loans. You can have short-term interest rates for long-term projects, without being required to pay back until five years after the project is open. This means until a project survives the first set of market risks, the developer can hold off paying the money back. You can restructure the debt over a 30-year period in lots of ways. But four years after ISTEA almost nothing has changed. Since 1991, I can think of maybe three Section 1012 loans that have been completed or are in negotiations, one for a bridge in Laredo, Texas, one for a highway in Texas, and another for a bridge in Florida. There may be others, but there are very few.

Not much imagination has been applied. The Transportation Control Agencies in Southern California managed to sell some $3 billion worth of bonds using an imaginative series of layers of financing, but such imagination is rare. A good question is why more hasn't happened. The simplistic answer is that there are no net new dollars. I find the concept of bribing people to do things that are good for them somewhat odd. There are, however, other reasons these concepts have not taken off. One is that these financial tools are complex and new to the somewhat conservative world of transportation. You are talking about lines of credit, loan guarantees, and soft loans. Also, you are talking to people who manage transportation agencies and have backgrounds either as engineers or planners. You get into fairly esoteric things that begin to sound a little bit like derivatives on top of a world in which they have to relate to the Clean Air Act, metropolitan planning organizations, and other things, and the pace of change is just too much for them to handle. A second reason for slow implementation of these new tools is the need for institutional changes. You cannot just plunk down a brilliant financing idea in the middle of an organization and treat it in isolation. You have to have a mechanism, which requires institutional change. So I would call that strike three.

It is not that I think the story is over. If you look back at last year's election, two major things happened that influenced transportation finance. First, if anyone ever needed evidence, the election proved the federal government will not be the savior in terms of future financing. Second, it proved there is openness to new ideas, not just at the federal level but at all levels of government.

The most tangible sign of this openness to new ideas in transportation has been what FHWA calls the Test and Evaluation-045 (TE-45) effort. TE-45 is an FHWA program that encourages experiments by relaxing existing federal rules. TE-45 focuses on state financial innovations. This is one of the most brilliant ideas I have heard. There is a provision in federal law that lets the FHWA, on an experimental basis, allow states to propose ideas that may contradict existing regulations. The idea is to develop better reinforcing bars, or better ways of building bridges, and so forth. Jane Garvey, Deputy Administrator for FHWA, and Steve Martin, Director of Innovative Finance for the U.S. Department of Transportation, applied this to finance. They said we will probably approve any financing idea you can come up with, as long as it is not illegal.

In the last year or so they have had more than 70 proposals from about 30 states, involving a whole range of things from cash flow improvements to leveraging to more flexible use of funds. It is an amazing range of ideas. In a sense it provides a test bed for the next ISTEA. Most important, it has stimulated thinking and action at the state level. However, no permanent financial mechanism exists. Ideas are scattered all over the place, and each one is different. Some states have submitted two or three proposals, but there is really no focus.

How can we implement more of these concepts? Is there a way to structure them? I think there are two answers. The first one is very simple, and that is to hire John Platt from the Ohio Department of Transportation. John Platt is my hero. He is in charge of innovative finance in Ohio and is trying to integrate half a dozen different approaches in the Ohio Department of Transportation. The projects involve everything from railroads to highways to intermodal facilities.

What other mechanisms are out there? Well, there are these things called infrastructure banks, which do not quite exist yet. They are the transportation version of revolving loan funds, which have been in existence for some time for wastewater treatment. Unlike wastewater treatment revolving funds, however, which were designed to get the federal government out of the wastewater treatment business, there are really no rules attached to these infrastructure banks. But there is a focus. How they are used and implemented will depend on the creativity of each state department of transportation.

The recently passed National Highway System Designation Act calls for 10 pilot projects for state infrastructure banks (SIB). Again, no new money has been appropriated, but there is clear recognition in Congress to do something different. The president's 1997 budget proposes $250 million for SIBs. In fact, in some ways this will be the first new idea that has come out of the new Congress relating to transportation. The neat thing about a SIB is that you can hang a lot of things on it. It is not just a way to make a soft loan; it is, in theory, a living financing tool. You can make soft loans to private or public firms, open lines of credit, work in impact fees, provide loan guarantees, or leverage public or private funds.

From the economic and planning perspectives, there are some very nice things to be said about SIBs. First, they allow subsidies. Remember, we are discussing public works that provide public benefits, and subsidies are not necessarily bad. In fact, in many cases, they are required to get projects started. Second, SIBs have a market orientation—something has to be paid back, whether it is a loan or line of credit, or whatever. Projects that benefit from an infrastructure bank must also pass a partial market test, which reduces the likelihood of building unnecessary projects.

Third, and this may be one of the most important thing to be said for SIBs, they encourage planners and decision makers to take a long-term view. One of the nice features of the bond market is you get paid back over 20 or 30 years. If you have a financial mechanism that is going to grow in strength over 20 years, you can focus political and planning power on making sure it works.

Fourth, SIBs are geared to help large projects. One of the biggest problems, in general, in infrastructure funding is that political pressures encourage programs that spread funding across as many jurisdictions as possible. It is awfully easy in most states to get money to resurface highways, for example. But to build something big, you must stop all the other programs in the state for a year, which means, politically, it does not happen.

Finally, SIBs offer a lot of flexibility. You can design them differently for Delaware than for Texas. You can make them suit whatever your local conditions are. Infrastructure banks are also multimodal. There is no requirement that as the money is repaid it must stay focused on a single mode.

I think the wave of the future will be a mix of innovative public and private sector funding. If you look at what states are doing in privatization, they are not following a Greenway model (which has proven painful for both the public and private sector). The states that are active in privatization now— Minnesota, Virginia, Delaware, South Carolina, and so forth—have different models. Minnesota, for example, says they will share risks with the private sector. They are going to kick in $2 million for predevelopment costs to help the private sector get projects going and $10 million a year to provide subsidies, if needed. The state of Florida is kicking in $70 million a year for the next 20 years for a private high-speed train because they know the project is not going to stand on its own.

Rather than a single national model, I think there will be a family of models, but with differences from state to state. The orientations will be different, but they will probably be flexible enough so they can change over time. In summary, I feel very optimistic about the future for infrastructure finance. I believe it will be better. It will also be different.

DISCUSSION

Several questions have been raised regarding the long term viability of the Highway Trust Fund for funding state revolving transportation funds as well its possible use in financing other forms of infrastructure.

I happen to believe that the Highway Trust Fund is a mechanism that is past its prime but which, over the years, has become somewhat more flexible. There is some transit money in it now. ISTEA, in particular, opened it up to being used for things that, at one point, were outside its scope. The fund has also been used to help reduce the federal budget deficit, but I think that impact has been exaggerated. There are certain proposals to move trust funds off budget and protect them but I worked at the Congressional Budget Office, and I know we would have figured a way to control an off-budget trust fund.

I think we need a new, more flexible model. When the interstate highway system was being talked about, the original proposal by President Eisenhower was to bond it. A number of people in the Congress, especially Senator Byrd from Virginia, advocated pay-as-you-go. As a result, today we have a mechanism that is a historical anachronism in the sense that it focuses on one system and one type of very conservative financing.

I think we need a set of new models that will be more flexible and, when appropriate, can issue bonds. The true pay-as-you-go concept is over the 20-year or 30-year life of projects. The new models need to be more flexible so that we can consider trade-offs, particularly within transportation, rather than considering highways the only answer.

I think we also need to decide on project-by-project basis what the most appropriate private sector role is. For this, you need a financial mechanism more open to new financial ideas. I do not know what will happen to the Highway Trust Fund. Ten years from now it could be a lot smaller. I think if you ignore political problems, you can make a good case for a publicly oriented infrastructure bank, if you will, that will allow flexibility for all types of infrastructure.

The Highway Trust Fund is politically important, so it will probably stay around. Some of the money that goes to the states from the fund could be used for infrastructure banks. People have talked in the past about turn-backs. The state of Ohio, wants, for example, to intercept part of the motor fuel tax for a multistate compact—something like corporatizing the Highway Trust Fund. I think one of the more interesting things to come from the last federal election is a new Congress with all sorts of new ideas. But they have yet to focus on infrastructure.

One current U.S. trend is for departments of transportation to talk with telecommunication companies because they want to use their rights of way for fiber-optic and other telecommunication systems. Some day you may find departments of transportation owning their own telecommunications systems. Georgia has a huge network for fiber-optics in all of its freeways because they need to get control of traffic for the Olympics. They have the motivation to go ahead and do some of these new things, which, if they had not had one big need, they would not have done for years. The lines between public and private are getting more mixed. If this is happening in the United States, where the model for infrastructure has been 100 percent public for such a long time, it is going to happen abroad as well. This is a somewhat chaotic time. Most of the time it is very exciting.

One dimension that has not been talked about at all is the indirect effects of highway investments, particularly as we push development further and further out to the periphery of metropolitan areas and leave behind impoverished urban cores. The poor in the center of the city, who still have to get to work, are having a hard time finding access to work.

The centers of many of our older urban areas represent a resource that is not being fully utilized. Michael Porter from the Harvard Business School has done some research that says there is significant economic value left behind in our urban cores. How we take advantage of that is another question. The state of Delaware is trying to implement some public/private legislation in a very different way. They are preparing to take bids from private firms to invest in transit or some urban-oriented intermodal facility as one possible option. That will require some subsidies, but the state department of transportation will also provide financial incentives for the private sector to put ideas and money in places we normally pass by. Most public/private projects around the country have been bridges or big toll roads because those are likely winners. There may be a different model out there that would help indirectly get at the issue you are talking about.

Looking at other infrastructure in this country, public surveys rarely find a negative reaction to water supplies being privately owned, per se. There is, however, often a negative reaction to having to pay for something the public used to think was free. That is the real problem to overcome. It is also clearly the trend in this country and around the world that more and more projects will fully depend on user fees, whether a project is sponsored by a private firm or public agency. In certain parts of the country, Orange County, California, perhaps, being private may actually help.

A broader change is that public infrastructure, in general, whether publicly or privately owned, will be operated more like a business. Private ownership is not necessarily a big negative. Paying for a toll road you did not have before is probably a bigger issue than whether it is privately or publicly owned. The privatization model going forward will look a lot like a public agency that acts like a business.

Perspective of the Investment Community

Ann L. Sowder
Government Finance Group, Inc.

I have been asked to reflect on the investment community perspective on infrastructure finance. First I want to give you a flavor of who comprises the investment community. Then I will move into a general discussion of new approaches to financing infrastructure in the United States. Not all of these approaches are new in the sense that they have been used for the first time in the last few years, but they are still new in many instances because they are not widespread. I will touch on some of the same examples the previous speaker mentioned, but I will put them in a different framework for us to consider.

Finally, I want to elaborate a little further on start-up toll roads in the United States. We have had several recent examples of large financing for these projects, a noteworthy development in terms of what is getting done in infrastructure finance, and they involve the investment community very intimately.

My first topic is who comprises the investment community. You have, on the one hand, debt investors. You heard General Williams mention the tiering of financing that underlies the Greenway project. He mentioned in that case short-term investors—bank financing—for construction and long-term lenders as part of their financing consortium. In the United States, in municipal finance, construction financing and long-term financing typically come as part of the same bond deal, and that is a distinction that is important to understand relative to the Greenway project. To some extent, I am going to use the Greenway project to draw some contrasts because it is so unusual. It is very different from most infrastructure projects in the United States that use public and private investment funds. Keep in mind that the Greenway project used taxable rate financing and that most public infrastructure financing in the United States uses tax exempt financing, which involves a whole different set of rules and players.

84

Debt investors receive a fixed return that is generally defined in terms of the timing of when they receive that return and fixed in terms of the rate of return. Among the debt side players, we have institutional investors. For the tax-exempt market, we are talking primarily about mutual funds. There are also individual retail investors, although most of the investment by retail investors these days is through the intermediary of mutual funds.

I would include on the debt side of financing rating agencies, which serve as proxies for investors and play a very important screening role in looking at projects. Rating agencies assign designations that rank the credit worthiness of various projects. To have access to mutual fund financing and access to retail investors for selling tax exempt bonds, the normal way to go is for a project to receive a rating. The rating must be above a certain threshold, which in the terminology used is "investment grade." That designation includes the AAA, AA, A, and BBB and Baa categories. These projects are the cream of the crop, although projects do get done that are not investment grade. But bigger projects, the ones we have seen lately that are attracting a lot of attention, have succeeded because they were designated investment grade. Rating agencies and how they look at projects are the first indicators of concerns that very much reflect what actual end investors are looking for.

We also have equity investors in projects, although in the kinds of projects that I am going to describe, equity investment is a bit of a misnomer or is not a major source of funding. Defining the difference between debt investment and equity investment can get a little fuzzy in the sense that highly subordinated debt lenders often, effectively, venture capitalist investors. That is the same sort of phenomenon we see in the corporate market where subordinate debt is really more akin to equity investment than to debt financing.

In the case of the Dulles Greenway, reference was made to equity investors. Another distinguishing factor of the Greenway project, which works against being replicated in great numbers, is that a lot of the willingness to contribute high-risk equity financing came from the expectation of related return on real estate owned by some of the parties in the immediate area. So, this was equity investment that is not typically what you think of as equity investment. It is not "stocks" in the normal sense of the word.

Another quasi-equity investment involvement that we see in financed infrastructure projects is contingent commitments, money put at risk (i.e., guaranteeing a commitment) from construction consortiums. This is a very important quasi-equity form of investment. It is especially important in the early stages of a project for getting the project to the point where you can attract publicly sold debt. Some of the projects I will refer to later had definite layers of construction-consortium committed capital, which were at the bottom of the totem pole of getting repaid but were absolutely critical to the success of those projects.

        With debt financing, you have debt investors, equity investors, and intermediaries between the sources of capital and the projects that need the capital, who are also considered part of the investment community. Investment bankers and financial advisors, such as my company, are intermediaries. We bring together projects and investors and work to structure financing so that the flow of capital from investors to projects takes place. The most important distinction between the investment banking community and financial advisory firms like mine is that investment banking firms are involved in actually underwriting, putting capital at risk, in order to sell the securities that make up the financing. Companies like the one I work for are not involved in the selling process of debt. We only advise on the planning and packaging of financing.

        That gives you an overview of who is included in the investment community because financing in the United States is primarily driven by cash flow and is not asset based. For the most part, the financing of infrastructure projects revolves around different types and different layers of debt financing, basically with fixed rates of return and a defined schedule by which the money is to be repaid.

        I want to reflect on how the investment community has been involved in infrastructure finance and the criteria they use in deciding which of the newer types of projects merit investment. Let me turn to some of the new approaches to financing infrastructure in the United States. There are two objectives underlying many of the approaches that are being used more frequently these days. The two objectives are, first, to use existing funds more effectively and, second, to attract new money, new investment funds for infrastructure. I want to review several of these techniques and categorize them along these lines. Essentially, are they taking existing money and trying to use it more effectively, or are they trying to get new money into the system?

        One option related to more efficient use of public funds is using loans rather than grants. The Environmental Protection Agency (EPA) state revolving fund program that was instituted in the mid-1980s is probably the prime example in the infrastructure finance area. This program represented a watershed change in the financing of wastewater facilities in the United States. It basically took a grant program and replaced it with a loan program. Injecting the financial discipline of repaying loans into the process has, based upon various studies and critiques of the program, been positive.

        One problem that remains is that under the old EPA program some communities could barely afford to come up with matching funds. If they could not afford the match before, they are certainly not in a position to repay loans now, and they are, in some cases, effectively left out of using loans as a financing option. But for most projects and communities, the loan program works because there is already a revenue stream in place, that is, water and sewer utility charges. Because there is a user fee that people are used to paying, it naturally feeds into using a loan mechanism.

Using loans rather than grants has introduced into the funding process recycling of capital, which that "stretches" money and uses it more effectively. Some of the state revolving loan programs have used debt to further increase the amount of money they have been able to lend out via the loan process. In general, various studies have found that the leveraging ratio is in the neighborhood of three to one, meaning agencies have been able to borrow funds roughly equal to three times the initial seed money (the equity contribution from the federal government). This is probably the prime example of using federal capitalization funds to replace grant programs and using a limited amount of money in a more effective way.

The infrastructure bank concept is very much under discussion presently. If it does not get through as part of the National Highway System Designation Act of 1995, you can expect that it will be back in the discussions of the reauthorization of ISTEA. The idea of making loans rather than grants for transportation financing is partly based on the experience of the EPA wastewater program. There is a real opportunity to do better when applying this concept to transportation. It will require a new way of thinking about highway projects because with most highway projects, as opposed to wastewater treatment projects, you do not have an existing ready-to-tap user fee revenue stream with which to repay loans. So, the concept will be harder to apply in the transportation area, but it promises more effective use of money in the federal trust fund which, for the most part, now goes out in the form of grants.

Another mechanism of using existing funds more effectively, stretching them, if you will, is federal lines of credit. However, this financing mechanism is available only in special cases at this time. Two large toll road financings in California had access to lines of credit from the federal government. Both the Foothill Eastern Toll Road Project and the San Joaquin Hills Project were done through transportation corridor agencies in Orange County. Each project has the ability to draw up to $120 million from the federal government to offset operating costs, shortfalls, or construction cost overruns and deficiencies. These lines of credit are available—in the case of the San Joaquin project—for five years after completion of construction and—in the case of Foothill Eastern—for 10 years after construction. The debt financing for these two projects did not rely, in terms of total repayment, on the lines of credit, but they were tangible evidence of federal support for these two very large, precedent-setting projects.

One rationale for having an infrastructure bank is the possibility of setting up the banks for transportation on a state or regional level using federal monies channeled through the states from the federal trust fund. Using those banks to provide lines of credit is one option.

Similar ideas for using state monies to enhance project financing can be found in a number of states, including Maryland and California, which already have state laws and mechanisms in place whereby localities have access to lower cost financing by diverting formula-distributed amounts from state transportation trust funds to pay debt service on bonds issued to finance local projects. This is an interesting parallel that has implications for transportation infrastructure banks, if they are set up, because it provides a ready stream of repayment money for projects and allows you to leverage. Several states are doing it, including Virginia, and I think more states will turn to it. It is a financing, or credit-enhancing, mechanism that is used widely for schools, for example. The opportunities for transportation are just now really being explored.

Moving from ways to use existing money more effectively to ways to raise new money, increased application of user fees is clearly the name of the game. Tolls, special assessments, and proffers are the primary ways this has been done in projects to date.

User fees in the transportation area do not necessarily mean only tolls on highways. One of the very interesting projects that John Platt from the Ohio Department of Transportation has put in place is an intermodal facility for transferring containerized cargo from trains to trucks and vice versa. A fee will be charged for use of the crane that transfers containerized cargo. This is, in effect, a toll on a different kind of activity. Mr. Platt is one of the most unconstrained in his thinking about how to find revenue streams. His philosophy is, basically, if there is a benefit, there may be a way you can charge for it. Then you can use that revenue stream to do a lot of different things. In this case, the up front financing for the crane, which is going to be at the heart of this intermodal facility, is coming by way of a loan from the state and will be, ultimately, funded in large part by federal funds. The loan will be repaid from user fees, the lift fee charged as part of this project.

With regard to start up toll road facilities, I will just make a few comments about special assessments and proffers. It is important to understand that, generally, special assessments as they are used and applied around the country are a recurring type of revenue stream that allow you to bond against the payments, which occur over time. Proffers, by contrast, are one-time, up front payments made at the time an occupancy permit or construction permit is given. Generally speaking, proffers can not be bonded against. They generally figure in as up front contributions to a project but do not figure into bond issues.

A second kind of effort to attract new investment funds into infrastructure investment is partnering. We have heard various references in the preceding discussions to public/private partnerships. We are also seeing a lot of public/public partnerships.

Public/private partnerships are really a mechanism for structuring transactions, which in and of itself is not going to attract private investment funds to a project. In order for private capital to be generated by a public/private partnership, you have to have a way for the private party to earn a rate of return. For the most part, that means having some sort of user fee. In the transportation context, that has generally meant a toll.

There is a lot of activity in this area. Private parties, such as construction consortiums, are interested in pursuing the right kind of projects and investing their own money up front in the planning. Once these projects get to a certain point, investors show increasing interest in and acceptance of investing in the debt sold to finance these projects. Some projects are public/public. In an increasing number of states, the toll authority is working with the state departments of transportation on projects with a degree of cooperation that has not been seen in the past. I think that departments of transportation working more closely with toll authorities is a trend we are going to see more of in the future.

In the last few years, more than $3.5 billion of investment capital has been contributed to four start up toll road projects alone: the two California projects I mentioned earlier, the Dulles Greenway, and the E-470 project in suburban Denver. E-470 is a loop road that goes almost all the way around the Denver area and will also serve the new Denver airport.

These projects have been accepted by the investment community and have received a tremendous amount of investment capital because of several characteristics they have in common. First and foremost has been a degree of public support. The commitment of local governments and state governments behind these projects and viewing them as alternative ways of providing transportation infrastructure not in competition with the state government, has been key to investor acceptance. A second element that has affected positive reaction from the investment communities relates to the nature of the projects. The two California projects relieved existing congestion, as distinct from the Dulles Greenway or even E-470, which were built more to spur and accommodate future growth. In general, investor reception has been stronger and more positive towards projects to relieve congestion because the users are already there. Other projects may get done, but at higher interest rates. They are harder to do.

Some other factors have increased investor acceptance. Construction guarantees have been critical to getting over the hurdle of the initial uncertainties of a project. Up front investment by construction consortiums with considerable financial wherewithal themselves has been key to investor acceptance. Also, computer modeling has advanced the science of making traffic and revenue forecasts, a critical area of expertise. But some of the projects financed with large deals have also greatly benefited from having small segments of the system already open, especially if projections were reasonably accurate for those segments. A lot of people will be watching projects like the Dulles Greenway to see how close the actual numbers come to projections. The success of many follow-on projects may be affected by how well the forecasters have done on the projects that have been financed to date. Finally, investors have reached a comfort level with increasing debt service schedules on these projects and using substantial reserves as part of the financing. That is a real watershed change, but it is a tangible indication of investor belief in these projects and the purposes they serve.

Taken all together, we see a lot of interest in financing infrastructure projects. If the projects that have been financed in the last few years turn out to be even reasonably successful, many more projects will be coming behind them. Investors and rating agencies have broadened their way of thinking about these projects, and there are new ways of getting things done. We think there will be more to come.

DISCUSSION

Participant: Do you know to what extent the landowners who participated in the Greenway project subjected their land to debt to generate money to buy the equity shares of the road? I question exactly whether it was a transportation project or a land development project. I was just wondering how much the two were interrelated.

Ms. Sowder: General Williams would be better able to give you some specifics on that. I do not know how the equity investors in that deal financed their contributions. I know some were personally very wealthy. Whether the others effectively took out loans on their property to help front that money, how that was secondarily financed, I am sorry I do not know.

I think your premise is right, though, that the deal was very real estate development driven. That deal would not have happened had there not been significant contributions of at-risk capital by those landowners. The tier of debt that goes ahead of that equity investment is from traditional lenders, insurance companies and pension funds. They got a very good rate of return on their investment.

The attempt to refinance that package prior to the opening of the road did not go through. I am not privy to all of the reasons, but I have to think that part of the reaction of the financial institutions was that they wanted to see actual use of the road before they agreed to take out some of the equity effectively and replace it with more debt financing.

Certainly Greenway has been a success story to this point in terms of the construction story, but the jury is still out on that road. It will be very interesting to watch. I get nervous about it, because I am fearful that so many other projects in the future may be adversely affected if Greenway does not play out well. I do not think that is necessarily a linkage because the Greenway project was so different.

Participant: A related question for Ms. Sowder. Early on, as U.S. companies tried to become involved in international private/public partnerships, many of the negotiations foundered on the concept of profit and compensation for risk. Have we seen the same thing here as these kinds of projects have been negotiated in the United States?

Ms. Sowder: That has not been the stumbling block. Fundamentally, the stumbling block for a lot of the public/private projects has been getting public support for the projects. We can look at the experience of five projects in California that are collectively referred to as the AB680 projects, which is a reference to Assembly Bill 680. The bill gave CalTrans, the state department of transportation in California, the ability to enter into franchise agreements that underlie several innovative projects that began five or six years ago or more. The bill allowed for negotiated rates of return on those projects.

Those projects are more like the projects that have followed, and they are fundamentally different from the Greenway project in this respect. Greenway fits a model that is typically referred to as "build, operate, transfer." General Williams talked about how the state gets the project back at the end of the 40-year franchise. The California roads were done in a mode that is typically referred to as "build, transfer, operate."

The private franchisee constructs the project, and then ownership of the project is turned over to the state. The state can enter into a lease agreement with the developer for operation of the project over a specified term, and the franchisee operator receives a negotiated rate of return. The operator has the flexibility to charge tolls. If they charge tolls that result in a rate of return in excess of the negotiated rate of return, the money has to be used either to retire debt or be given back to CalTrans. That is the approach California used.

Washington state, which embarked upon a very high-profile public/private process over a year ago, also started with the idea of negotiating rates of return. Virginia, which has just begun a new public/private project solicitation process, has set up the process so they can negotiate the rate of return on a project-by-project basis. Virginia is using a very different approach the second time than was used with Greenway, which had to go through the State Corporation Commission. That was basically a utility model of regulation.

The jury is still out on public acceptance of a given rate of return being earned on these projects. I have heard comments regarding the State Route 91 Project in Southern California, which involves charging tolls for using a high-occupancy vehicle lane in the middle of the Riverside Freeway, that this project might be too successful and earn too much for private sector investors, possibly hurting public acceptance of similar projects in the future. So we really have not gotten to the point yet where we have seen actual operations of some of these big, high-profile projects. That will be an interesting one to watch.

In Washington state, as I said, the problem affecting many projects is building public support for them. These projects have not gone forward far enough to test the rate-of-return aspect of the negotiation. They ran into a lot of public acceptance problems because of public resistance to tolls. Almost all of the projects there relied in some way on tolls.

From what I understand, there was also some resistance that arose from the fact that when you were dealing with private parties on these proposals there was, and I think rightfully so, attention paid to the confidentiality of information and proposals. The public, however, felt shut out of the review process. I think for the most part that is an unfair criticism, but often perception is reality. A lot of the public resistance has been more directed towards the idea of charging tolls and how projects are selected. There will be more projects to come, so we will have more examples to look at in the future. But only a few projects so far have gotten far enough along to get public reaction to negotiations on the rate of return. For the most part, these have been between state departments of transportation, local sponsors, and private consortiums.

Participant: One concern I have, maybe an issue that relates to similar public/private partnerships, is that politicians tend to make decisions on a short-term basis. Landowners are looking at the long-term benefits. I am thinking of the case of a regional airport or tollways running to a certain location. If private interests or long-term profits could influence the location of an infrastructure facility or a tollway or whatever, that would not necessarily be in the public's best interest on a long-term basis. But it might influence politicians on a short-term basis to accomplish something.

Ms. Sowder: Certainly that tension is there. I will fall back on some of the lessons learned from the experience with the two recent California toll roads. These projects were so big that even though the state had originally identified them, there was no prospect of funding them for many years to come. In California, the legal mechanism is joint action agencies. So a consortium of Orange County and cities in that area decided to pursue the project themselves.

Both projects were so expensive that they could not be built without a lot of help from the state. I do not mean just financial help. We talked about the federal line of credit, which is an indication of federal support for these kinds of projects. They were very big and originated out of state-identified plans that were not really susceptible to being driven by developers, albeit the Irvine Company in Orange County was very involved. They had a significant real estate interest and stood to benefit from spin-off development from both roads. Certainly their political persuasion should not be underestimated. These are examples where the local jurisdictions decided that they were going to step up to bat and make these projects happen because they did not see the money coming from the state.

On a smaller scale, there have been projects that, in retrospect, everyone agrees were too heavily influenced by particular developers. The history of special district financing is littered with situations where inappropriate projects were built—situations of excessive or inappropriate borrowing, of districts where the board was composed of appointees so the relative distribution of voting power was divided up by land ownership and a single developer could basically drive the decision to issue debt, of debt issuance running absolutely amok, far beyond the capacity of what the area could support.

There are also many examples of private development interests using the process to get debt issued that, sometimes, could not be repaid because development slowed down. The celebrated abuses of this process have resulted in reforms in many of the states that first used these financing mechanisms. Other states, particularly when they have looked at special district financing, have learned from these successes and failures. Now there is a body of experience that can help state and local governments set up a process—a lot has to do with governance issues as well as debt capacity—to make appropriate use of the user-pay mechanism without totally skewing priorities for projects.

Dr. McDowell: Let me give you another example. I was out in Las Vegas, which of course is a unique city. I did not realize until I got there that it has a population of one million people. In the next 7 to 10 years, they are looking at another million on top of that, which probably makes them the fastest growing place in the country. You know the place is dominated by one industry. It also has a lot of people out there in business who like to make decisions one day and act on them the next.

Well, they have a substantial transportation problem, a lot of it in the casino corridor. The federal transportation planning requirements say that when you have a problem like that you have to do a major investment study. It lays out the whole multiyear process. They are about a year into it, and it is going to take two more years. The city has started solving this transportation problem, and they have invited casino owners to be a part of the process along with others from the community. The casino owners sit there and nod their heads, but they do not give input.

One of the owners already has built a one-mile monorail to connect two of his casinos. Another casino owner decided he wanted a direct connection to the airport, so he was going to build it. What stopped him was not government but the other casino owners who decided this owner would have an unfair advantage. In the remaining two years of the planning process, government does not know what to do because the planners are afraid the transportation system will be built before it is planned. The bottom line is that the required public process is too slow to respond to this dynamic situation.

The only thing they have made any headway on is trying to convince casino owners that they should look not just at the casino attendees, the resort people who are being attracted, but also at their employees' needs. That idea has begun to sink in a little bit, but aside from that, casino owners are really pretty much on their own track.

Mr. Tischler: Maryland has been working for several years on a major investment study for the multi-million-dollar U.S. 301 corridor project. They requested consultants on a volunteer basis to review their projections because obviously land use projections drive the planning assumptions. We found that they had forecast the District of Columbia to expand by, I believe it was 188,000 jobs between 1990 and the year 2015. In fact, so far during the 1990s, the District has lost jobs. However, regardless of the actual numbers—perhaps the District will add 50,000 jobs—the point is population projections developed by the Metropolitan Planning Organizations, i.e., the Washington Council of Governments, must be used for project planning. Those of you who have worked on population forecasts know how political that process is.

My point is that millions of dollars are spent on these major investment studies which require several years to complete, and in the case of the 301 corridor, result in transportation alternatives based on an unrealistic set of employment projections. This generates a planning scenario of light rail linked to Metro by express buses using dedicated lanes when, in reality, the situation will be far different. So now these people have been in the process for two years, and maybe they have to go back to the drawing board. It is very frustrating for both the citizens who are participating in this project and the private sector.

Solutions for Local Government

Paul S. Tischler
Tischler and Associates

I want to talk about three areas: finance and accounting, planning, and revenue.

In the area of finance and accounting there are some realities, some of which may be obvious but are worth noting. In many jurisdictions, the infrastructure *replacement* costs are significantly greater than the need for *new* infrastructure. Increasingly in a community that is growing, the emphasis is on new because the community is already getting behind.

The second point about finance and accounting is that infrastructure costs are usually only about 10 to 20 percent of a jurisdiction's budget. In fact, the associated *operating costs* are usually more significant than capital costs. Our firm has been involved in several cases where the jurisdiction decided to postpone opening a new facility that was almost finished in order to avoid paying operating costs. For example, although the cost of building a fire station and providing the apparatus can be significant, the annual operating costs of full-time firefighters dwarf the annual capital costs. It is always interesting when I go to local communities that the discussion of retrofitting a facility or adding a modular addition takes up more time in public hearings than the operating expenses, fringe benefits, and other things that really eat up budgets.

The last point about finance and accounting is that it is surprising, when you think about it, that most jurisdictions do not have a depreciation account. Most private sector enterprises have a depreciation account for capital assets. That is, as a facility ages, the company sets aside money for replacement. In the public sector, water and sewer utilities routinely budget for replacement. Unfortunately, except for utilities, most jurisdictions do not maintain depreciation accounts. No money is set aside, and most older communities, consequently, are facing a "time bomb" when it comes to rehabilitating or replacing existing capital facilities. That means a community meeting capital facility needs arising from demands from growth, and there are very few of those, is not addressing at all the needs for the remaining useful life of existing infrastructure. The cities are the worst examples of that.

Two exceptions are cities we worked with that did establish capital facility replacement funds—Plymouth, Minnesota, and Germantown, Tennessee. Both jurisdictions had common characteristics of progressive leadership and citizens interested in their physical future. But they are almost unique among cities. In growing jurisdictions, operating costs must also be evaluated. In older communities, funding the replacement of existing facilities must be addressed.

In the area of planning, most jurisdictions are operating under such severe fiscal constraints now that they are just concerned about meeting the current operating needs of their jurisdiction, not about aggressive long-term capital improvement program (CIP) budgets.

The availability of basic infrastructure, such as water, sewers, and roads, opens up areas to new development. On the other hand, new development in an area generates the need for more capital facilities and equipment, such as schools, parks, libraries, police cars, and fire and rescue equipment. Unfortunately, when projected revenues are not sufficient to meet expenditures, the CIP suffers. Invariably, if a jurisdiction needs to save money, it may freeze vacancies but will not lay off staff. Instead, the six-year CIP will be postponed, again. This results in continuing backlogs for needed infrastructure.

Postponing capital facilities is likely to decrease the level of service, a key problem of infrastructure. For example, many communities have adopted comprehensive land-use plans. However, providing needed roads recommended in the plan can not keep pace with growth. The result is a deterioration in the level of service for existing and new residents.

In addition to the decrease in the existing level of service, there is another phenomenon. This is the level of "service creep." Service creep has generated greater (little understood) impacts on communities than the effects of new growth. For example, statistical studies show that there are more cars per capita, more trips per car, and more vehicle miles driven per car than there were five years ago. As a result, the same population generates an increased demand for roads to maintain the same level of service.

Another example is schools in Baltimore County, Maryland. We were hired by the chamber of commerce in Baltimore County to find out how Baltimore County schools got in the position they were in and what to do about it. Schools and transportation are the two major local infrastructure issues, and schools are more influential in land-use decisions and movement, etc., than transportation. Home builders did not want to be shut down and were being threatened with a moratorium on schools.

What created this conflict was postponing necessary construction and service creep. Beginning in the 1980s, Baltimore County did not want to raise taxes or expand schools. Ten to fifteen years later the number of students in the school district was the same, but the requirement for classrooms had almost doubled. The reason was the increased level of service—fewer children per classroom, required special education and other programs, and electives local residents wanted to implement in the school system. The impact is not only on the size of classrooms, but also on operating expenses, additional teachers, etc.

The solution was to reduce the level of service. They could not afford the level of service because they did not have the debt capacity to build that many schools and they did not want to raise taxes. We said they had to increase the number of pupils in the class because otherwise the situation was hopeless. When this hit the front page of the *Baltimore Sun*, the Parent Teacher Association president was quoted as saying, "They were not asked to look at level of service. That is crazy." The next year they, in fact, had to reduce the level of service by adding two pupils to each class. Relatively few residents understand this phenomenon. They assume the shortage of infrastructure is due to new growth and not to increasing demands for service by existing residents.

That is an example of how levels of service change, which, to me, is the major reason jurisdictions cannot afford to operate and meet the challenges of growth. A sidebar of that example is the development community in Baltimore County, who said, they were willing to pay their fair share, willing to pay impact fees. That is the first example I know of where a development group proposed paying impact fees so they could build.

Another planning issue is that infrastructure can significantly influence new development patterns. That point is obvious. But the fourth point under planning issues is very important. Infrastructure costs generally increase as density decreases, what I call "cost of sprawl." The tendency of infrastructure costs to increase as density decreases is only part of the financial picture. This gets us into revenue issues, an entry into the next topic and the third area I want to talk about.

To find out the impact of infrastructure on a community, you have to do a fiscal analysis, which can be defined as cash flow to the public sector. To analyze cash flow, you look at all the revenues, all the operating expenses, and the capital costs. Very few jurisdictions are doing this kind of fiscal impact evaluation.

Howard County, Maryland, is an example of the cost of sprawl concept. In the state of Maryland, income tax reverts to the county government, there are transfer taxes, and there are substantial property taxes. Those three components are critical revenue ingredients in Howard County. Because of this structure, revenues accruing from higher valued housing with higher incomes more than offset the infrastructure costs of low-density development. From a fiscal perspective, low-density development makes more sense than high-density development even though the infrastructure costs are greater. Any of you dealing with local communities should be aware of this "opposite" result, which is not evident from just looking at infrastructure.

The methodology for a fiscal impact analysis should be a case study-marginal cost approach, versus a per capita average cost approach. The per capita average cost approach to a fire department budget, for example, would divide the budget by population to arrive at a per capita cost. This per capita cost would be the same regardless of the spatial distribution or timing of new developments. In contrast, a case study-marginal cost approach would consider the fire department's response time to serve a new development. It would also consider whether existing fire stations could serve the new development or whether a new fire station should be built. An example is the addition of 1,000 homes in somewhat of an in-fill situation, versus 1,000 homes in a leap-frog situation. The former would probably generate no additional costs in constant dollars. The latter would probably necessitate a new fire station, apparatus, and annual staffing costs.

In many jurisdictions, the costs of new capital facilities and other services are greater than projected revenues from new development. One reason for this is a decrease in state and federal funding at the same time that both voluntary or required mandates have been imposed raising the required level of service. Because elected officials are reluctant to raise property taxes, new funding approaches are needed. By conducting a fiscal impact analysis, a jurisdiction can focus on how development and the provision of infrastructure and related operating costs will affect the need for additional revenues.

Little Rock, Arkansas, is an example of what is happening throughout the country. Little Rock, unfortunately, is a case of both cost of sprawl and level of service creep. Little Rock annexed and doubled in size in the 1980s. In older areas of the city, the infrastructure is deteriorating because money was not being put into the older community. People in the older areas felt they were being neglected and that new growth was sapping the resources of the city. On the other hand, developers felt they were paying their way with revenues generated from new growth. We looked at the fiscal impact of development. Every community is unique, but in the case of Little Rock we found that new development did in fact pay for itself. The major reasons this was true were the market value of new housing, the relatively low level of service, and the fact that the developers had to build capital facilities.

Then we looked at why the infrastructure quality of life was deteriorating in older parts of the city. We looked at the cost of disinvestment in older parts of the city, as far as I know the first time this has been studied. The cost of disinvestment is a very important issue that large cities need to address more than they do. Older portions of the city were losing residents. People wanted to move out of the city or into larger housing. They did not have any more debt in their houses. The housing values were not very high (it is a low-cost city). They basically were giving their houses away.

The costs of disinvestment to the city are loss of revenue, loss in assessed value, which translates directly to property taxes; and an increase in costs. The city incurs direct costs for community-oriented police, housing inspectors, street lighting, animal control, arson investigation, judicial activities, and demolition of housing units. The city loses revenues as units are demolished and existing units decrease in value.

The point is that the cost of disinvestment far surpasses the net revenues from new development. Does that mean you should stop new development? No, because people will go elsewhere, across the city lines. By the way, the city of Little Rock is attracting 80 percent of the employment base in the whole metropolitan area, and you still see these results. So the city is now engaged in revitalizing the downtown and older neighborhoods. We provided them with examples of successful redevelopment from other cities throughout the country.

Even Boise, Idaho, a city that is growing, has fiscal problems. We just looked at development scenarios in Boise. I suspect most people would think of Boise as a healthy city. In all of the growth alternatives, we showed that new growth generated a need for $4 million to $5 million a year extra out of other city revenues. Boise cannot even afford to meet capital improvement replacement programs. So even a city like Boise, which does not have many of the urban problems you find in the eastern half of the country, has fiscal problems.

I believe that there are solutions to local financing, and they are quite simple. The mechanisms are there to increase sales taxes, gasoline taxes, and income taxes. I am talking about a quarter or half of one percent. The base is so large that those dollars coming back to the community can be substantial. Unfortunately, most states do not want to authorize localities to even put tax increases on the ballot.

There are various possible approaches to either accommodating or curbing the need for infrastructure. Some of these are revenue mechanisms. These could include:

- special or assessment districts
- private financing
- impact fees
- developer contributions/agreements
- revenue bonds
- real estate taxes
- real estate transfer taxes

Other, nonrevenue approaches could curb or monitor the need for new infrastructure. These include adequate public facilities ordinances and transfer of development rights ordinances that make it possible to reassign development intensities from low density areas to areas where growth is desired.

Transfer of development rights provide some flexibility on certain things. I talked with previous speaker Ms. Sowder about "takings," or legislative actions that are confiscatory. Taking issues are a concern now in Congress. The issues around compensation for property owners for regulatory actions will put a damper on planning department efforts to become or remain aggressive. But there is no corresponding discussion about what is given. If you have to pay somebody the value of the land you are taking, then what about infrastructure improvements on behalf of landowners? They are being given something. Well, it might make sense to talk about that half of the equation, too, and trace a transfer of development rights.

Impact fees raise several issues that are symptomatic of what is happening today. First, there is the intergenerational equity issue. We paid or our parents paid for infrastructure for us, but we are no longer willing to pay for infrastructure for our children, or at least not the full bill. This is a dramatic change. I think it is due largely to not understanding the level of service creep.

In some communities developers have been told, "You want to fight us in the state legislature to implement impact fees? That is all right. We are going to implement an adequate public facilities ordinance, which means unless we have capacity for new development, we are not going to allow it to be authorized." There have been several states where that threat has been made, and they have allowed the new revenue exaction of impact fees.

By the way, the National Association of Homebuilders has not come out against impact fees. The reason is that responsible builders realize that— because of cutbacks in federal and state funds and the timidity of local officials about raising taxes—there have to be other revenue sources. Impact fees require a rigorous process on the part of jurisdictions to come up with a justifiable fee structure. Developers have a certain amount of time to pay and develop, and they know the money is going to be spent for new development.

An example of a special agreement, like a special assessment district, is Douglas County, Colorado, just south of Denver, which had school impact fees. The case was thrown out of court, but developers "volunteered" to pay impact fees, even though they did not have to because they were worried they might not otherwise get approval from the local jurisdiction.

In conclusion, I think there is a lack of education of the public about what has happened in providing services. People do not understand the cost to a police department of having officers handle child abuse cases, for example. It is the same with education. One child more or one less per class has a ripple effect on the level of service and on infrastructure costs. By fully understanding the capital costs, operating expenses, and revenue sources available to a jurisdiction, a community can better understand how it can meet the demands of new growth and maintain the level of service to current residents. By going through this process, the community will also be "educated" on the need to budget for replacing existing infrastructure.

Until people are better educated, there will continue to be a ripple effect of a lack of confidence in government. Until the basic lack of confidence in government is overcome, there is going to be great reluctance to allow more revenues to jurisdictions to pay for their needs. If localities do not have the revenue mechanisms they need to solve these problems, we will fall further behind in providing necessary infrastructure, which will ultimately lead to decreases in the levels of service.

Biographical Sketches of Colloquium Participants

George Bugliarello is chancellor of Polytechnic University, chairman of the Board on Infrastructure and the Constructed Environment of the National Research Council and a member of the National Academy of Engineering. He has chaired the Board on Science and Technology for International Development of the National Academy of Sciences, the Advisory Committee for Science and Engineering Education of the National Science Foundation, and has consulted on numerous international assignments. Dr. Bugliarello chairs the Metrotech Corporation, established by Polytechnic University to create Metrotech (a university-industry park in New York City). He holds a doctor of science degree in engineering from Massachusetts Institute of Technology and has been awarded several honorary degrees.

Timothy J. Brennan is a professor of policy sciences and economics at the University of Maryland Baltimore County Campus and senior fellow at Resources for the Future in Washington, D.C. His research has been focused on regulatory economics, antitrust, and numerous information issues, including regulating broadcasting, the First Amendment, and copyright. In addition, he has published papers on the ethics and philosophy of economics. His articles have appeared in journals specializing in economics, philosophy, communications, and law. Among his current research topics are regulatory "takings," structure of the telecommunications market, deregulating electricity, privacy, measuring environmental damage, and the role of moral rights in making public policy. Dr. Brennan has a Ph.D. in economics and a M.A. in mathematics from the University of Wisconsin.

Natalie R. Cohen is president of New York-based National Municipal Research and publisher of Fiscal Stress Monitor, a monthly publication that analyzes regional and local trends affecting the fiscal condition of state and local governments. The publication was launched in the fall of 1994 and includes a subscriber base of rating agencies, bond insurers, commercial banks, broker/dealers, money managers, academics, government officials and the press. Ms. Cohen's more than 15 years of experience in the municipal industry includes rating credits at Moody's Investors Service in the Public Finance Department and supervising the planning of New York City's $8 billion education budget at the New York City Office of Management and Budget. She is a member of the National Federation of Municipal Analysts, the Municipal Analysts Guild of New York, and the Municipal Forum and has been a member of the Public Securities Association Credit Research Committee. Ms. Cohen has a B.A. degree from Hampshire College in Massachusetts and an M.P.A degree from the Robert F. Wagner School of Public Service at New York University.

Nancy Connery is a private consultant, author, and lecturer on public investment, management, and infrastructure issues and a member of the Board on Infrastructure and the Constructed Environment of the National Research Council. She is the former executive director of the National Council on Public Works Improvement and serves as advisory editor and contributor to The Public's Capital, an infrastructure newsletter published jointly by Harvard University and the University of Colorado, Denver. Ms. Connery has received the Silver Hard Hat Award from the Construction Writers' Association, Distinguished Service Award from American Public Works Association, and the Rebuilding America Award from CIT Group/Equipment Finance. She received a masters degree of public administration, as a Lucius Littauer Fellow from the John F. Kennedy School of Government, Harvard University, and a bachelor of arts cum laude in political science from Pacific Lutheran University.

Carol Everett is the director of special programs for the American Public Works Association (APWA). She is responsible for managing and developing special projects of longer duration than projects normally undertaken by the organization. In 1992, Ms. Everett was named the executive director for the Rebuild America Coalition, which is a broad coalition of 60 public and private organizations committed to reversing the decline in America's investment in infrastructure. Ms. Everett has a master's degree in economics from the University of Wisconsin.

Frannie Humplick is an infrastructure economist in the Policy Research Department at the World Bank. Her current responsibilities include managing research on infrastructure, keeping abreast of policy changes in infrastructure around the world, and advising governments on infrastructure expenditures and sector reform. She is an associate editor of the Journal of Infrastructure Systems and a member of various committees on infrastructure related issues. Dr.

Humplick holds a M.S. in transportation systems and a Ph.D. in infrastructure systems from Massachusetts Institute of Technology.

Bruce McDowell is director of government policy research at the Advisory Commission on Intergovernmental Relations in Washington, D.C. He has been with the commission 1963–1964, 1972–1986, and 1988–present, where his interests have included federal urban development programs, substate regionalism, regional transportation, citizen participation, the federal aid system, and intergovernmental consultation processes. On 1986-88, Dr. McDowell was on the staff of the National Council on Public Works Improvement. Dr. McDowell has lectured at numerous colleges and universities and was on the faculty of the Salzburg Seminar in American Studies in 1977 and the International Conference on Urban Planning and Economics in Beijing, China, in March 1988. Dr. McDowell is active in numerous planning and public management associations. He holds bachelor and doctoral degrees from American University and the master of city planning degree from the Georgia Institute of Technology.

Richard R. Mudge is president of Apogee Research, a firm that specializes in economics, finance, and policy aspects of public works. He is a nationally known expert in the economics and finance of environmental and transportation infrastructure. Dr. Mudge has made numerous appearances as an expert witness before the U.S. Congress and has extensive experience with infrastructure finance and the economic value of public works. He holds a Ph.D. in regional economics from the University of Pennsylvania and received his undergraduate degree from Columbia College.

Ann L. Sowder is vice president at Government Finance Group, Inc. She has more than 15 years of experience in municipal finance, including financial advisory work, underwriting, and rating agency experience. Since joining Government Finance Group in 1994, Ms. Sowder has directed and coordinated transportation-related financial advisory and consulting assignments. Ms. Sowder is a chartered financial analyst. Ms. Sowder is a graduate of the Woodrow Wilson School of Princeton University, with a masters in public affairs, and the University of Virginia, where she earned a bachelor of arts in economics.

Paul S. Tischler is principal of Tischler & Associates, Inc, a fiscal, economic, and planning consulting firm with a national practice. Mr. Tischler has been retained by dozens of public and private sector clients in roles ranging from project manager to expert witness. The firm concentrates in the following areas: fiscal impact analyses; evaluation of impact fees; capital facility forecasting; and economic and market studies. Mr. Tischler is the chair, Economic Development Division of American Planning Association, is listed in Who's Who in Real Estate, Who's Who in Finance and Business, and Who's Who in the East. He received his MBA in real estate and urban development from American University and a bachelor of arts in economics from Johns Hopkins University.

Charles E. Williams is executive vice president and chief operating officer of Rebuild Incorporated. He is the former chief operating officer of the Toll Road Investors Partnership II where he was responsible for managing the construction of the Dulles Greenway. A retired major general of the U.S. Army Corps of Engineers, he has more than 30 years of financial and construction management experience. He is an adjunct professor of the Byrd School of Business, Shenandoah University, a member of the Board of Trustees at Shenandoah University and the Board of Directors of the Loudoun Hospital. In addition to being a graduate of both the Army basic and advanced engineering schools and the Army War College, he holds an MBA, which is supplemented by the Kennedy School of Government Senior Managers Program at Harvard University.

Deborah L. Wince-Smith is currently a senior fellow at the Council on Competitiveness, a nonprofit coalition of chief executives from leading businesses, academia, and organized labor dedicated to improving the competitiveness of U.S. industry and raising the standard of living in America. She was the first assistant secretary for technology policy in the Department of Commerce and a senior fellow at the Congressional Economic Leadership Institute, a nonprofit foundation providing a neutral forum to discuss with members of Congress and the private sector key issues affecting America's economic vitality. Ms. Wince-Smith is a member of advisory boards, councils, and boards of directors of leading national organizations and U.S. firms, such as the National Security Advisory Board of Los Alamos National Laboratory and the Association of Technology Business Councils. Trained in classical archeology, Ms. Wince-Smith did anthropological field work in Pakistan, India, and Afghanistan. She graduated Phi Beta Kappa and magna cum laude from Vassar College and received her masters degree from Cambridge University.